Crime and Disorder in Late Georgian Alfriston

W H Johnson

Downsway Books

First published in 1994 by
DOWNSWAY BOOKS
58 Berkeley Court, Wilmington Square,
Eastbourne, East Sussex BN21 4DX

Reprinted in 2005

Copyright W H Johnson 1994

All rights reserved

Typeset by MCM, Alfriston
In Century 702pt PS

Printed & bound by
Antony Rowe Ltd, Eastbourne

British Library Cataloguing in Publication Data

A catalogue record for this book is available
from the British Library

ISBN 0 9518564 4 8

Foreword	5
Backcloth	11
Unutterably banal ..... stultifying ordinariness	18
Some Crimes, 1822 - 1825	27
The Alfriston Disorders, 1825 - 1828	28
Some Crimes, 1826 - 1828	38
Some Cases of Arson, 1827 - 1831	39
Some Crimes, 1830 - 1831	45
The Trials of Collins and Awcock, 1831	47
The Events of Sunday, 11th December 1831:	57

The 'Riot' in the Chapel
    Attempted Arson at Brooker's Warehouse
    The Fire at Milton Court Farm	

The Trial of Samuel Thorncraft, 1832	63
Some Crimes, 1832 - 1833	73
Poor Law, Workhouse and Fire, 1834 - 1835	75
Some Crimes, 1834 - 1837	83
Conclusion	87
Notes on Locations	90
Sources	93

ILLUSTRATIONS

The Parsonage Barn, Alfriston, S H Grimm, 1787   43

REWARD NOTICES

Reward Notice : Milton Street fire, 1831   61

Reward Notice : Frog Firle fire, 1834   81

MAPS

Section of Sussex, Margary and Phillimore, 1825   10

Hand-drawn Map, 1832 Trial   68

FOREWORD

I have been prompted to write this account of crime and disorder in late Georgian Alfriston largely because no-one else has tried to do it. Indeed, the whole history of the village has been neglected and what records there are have been conspicuously ignored. Some of those who have attempted to offer accounts of early nineteenth century Alfriston have presented the reader with a mishmash of folk-myth and faulty historical fiction. This then is an attempt to respond to the need to record a brief passage of the history of a Sussex village as accurately as possible and to remedy some of the distortions of others who have pretended to tell it.

I have wanted for some time to write down the known facts of Stanton Collins' career. His is the one name out of the village's past of which people might have heard. He is its romantic smuggler or at least, he is alleged to have been. That much of what has been written about him is at best dubious is enough justification for my offering a nearer approximation to the truth. My present researches have also allowed me to introduce more material about Charles Brooker to whom I devoted some space in an earlier book. Brooker, a man of great ability and great humanity, deserves to be better known. He is a significant figure in the history of the village.

I have focused deliberately upon a very short time-span. The frontiers of late Georgian England may be open to dispute. Whilst some would start in 1800, I have located the close of the Georgian period somewhere in the post-1815 years when the situation of the labouring poor had already deteriorated and when, for a variety of reasons, there was considerable unrest throughout the country. My first example of a criminal offence is, therefore, in 1822. I close with crimes in 1837, the year of Victoria's accession. Perhaps there will be a quibble. Was William IV, reigning from 1830 till 1837, a Georgian? I say he was and there seem to be no good reasons for denying it.

Whilst the title may imply that the account is confined to Alfriston, either the village or the parish, in my narrative I frequently refer to occurrences in neighbouring parishes and hamlets. Generally, none of the places I mention - except perhaps Folkington and Jevington - is more than a forty-minute walk from the village. And of the time I write, those living in the parishes of Lullington, Litlington, Berwick and the Milton Street end of Arlington, tended to look to Alfriston as their centre. After all, Alfriston was larger than those other places; it had some shops and industries; it offered some employment; and even though they relied on the pedlar and the packman for much of their needs, people outside came also to Alfriston for some of their purchases.

Many of the buildings mentioned in the text can be seen today although some have changed their use: Deans Place Farm is now an hotel and Brooker's tannery now serves as two houses. The barn set on fire at Milton Court in 1831 has also been converted to residential use. The National School which was nearly engulfed by fire when an arsonist struck at the Parsonage Barn, is now the village hall. But of The Royal Oak, the public house across the river, and the cottages next to it, not a stone remains.

But why crime and disorder? Why bother to write about that, the rough underside of rural life?

Or perhaps, why crime and disorder and intolerable poverty?

Why not? If the past is to be revealed, its backcloth of misery and unfairness cannot remain hidden. Along with the timeless turn of the farming year, the season's demand for ploughing, sowing and harvesting, there trudged generations of men, women and children, in deepest want. Bewildered by the contrast between the richness of the land and the rewards it offered to some, and their own crushing poverty, they had little hope for betterment of their condition. Alfriston, a tourist haunt today, charms its visitors; it seduces them, perhaps, into a belief that the past, quaint and picturesque, has been preserved. But the past was not like this. It was not chocolate box. It was not neat, ordered, repaired, fresh painted.

The past was grim for many. The crimes which litter the period were not romantic nor were those who committed them. Neither were the offenders always bad, any more so than many of their crimes.

But there were bad men - mainly men - who committed crimes.

And undoubtedly, good ones too. This book is an attempt to record what offences they committed and to suggest some of the reasons for them.

ACKNOWLEDGEMENTS

I am most grateful to Mary Catt who sent me information about her ancestor, Stanton Collins. I am sorry that I cannot portray him in a more sympathetic light. I also acknowledge the kindness of Joyce Cooper who responded to my newspaper letter asking for information about Collins.

On my visit to the Public Record Office, Chancery Lane, I was helped considerably by John Baker. My thanks to him. I am also indebted to Julian Tayler and my wife, Anne, for their appraisals of the draft manuscript.

I ought also to make specific mention of Roger Wells whose fascinating article, 'Popular Protest and Social Crime' in Southern History Vol 13, encouraged me to follow up this topic.

Sometimes, some summer mornings, the caps of the Downs float like islands in a sluggish, milky sea. Only when the mists clear is there any definition. Then, the diamond-bright day lights up the creamy fields of barley and the tan ploughlands which flank the greens of pasture, scrub and high-up slopes where once the myriad flocks trod burnet and trefoil, thyme, yarrow and eyebright. Across the valley's sides the trackways lead to Jevington and Eastbourne or to Bo-peep, Lewes and beyond, along the whole length of the Downs and into Hampshire. Below, the road which has come with some urgency over from the Weald keeps distant company with the river for a while until it has to snake its separate way over Hindover and on to Seaford.

Berwick's spire and Lullington's squat church are landmarks here as is the huddle of houses that is Litlington. There is pink-washed Milton Court and further on, just half a mile, is the white bridge spanning the Cuckmere. And then on the other side of the water there is Alfriston, with the confidently random contours of its roofs, their pinks and browns, oranges and ochres, that are among the glories of the old place.

This is a Saxon-named village, surrounded by parishes and villages with Saxon names. There are fields about here called Pingle and Goslings, Meg Meadow and Egle's Brook, Quinnyers and Appleton. You might think it a land of poets. Here is the ribbon of the river that once persuaded men to believe that Alfriston was a port. And this is the place where Collins and Brooker hated each other. Here men maimed animals, stole corn and sheep and damaged property sometimes out of anger, too often out of need. This is the country where young Thorncraft burnt the barn that lit his way to the gallows in a harsh and bitter time.

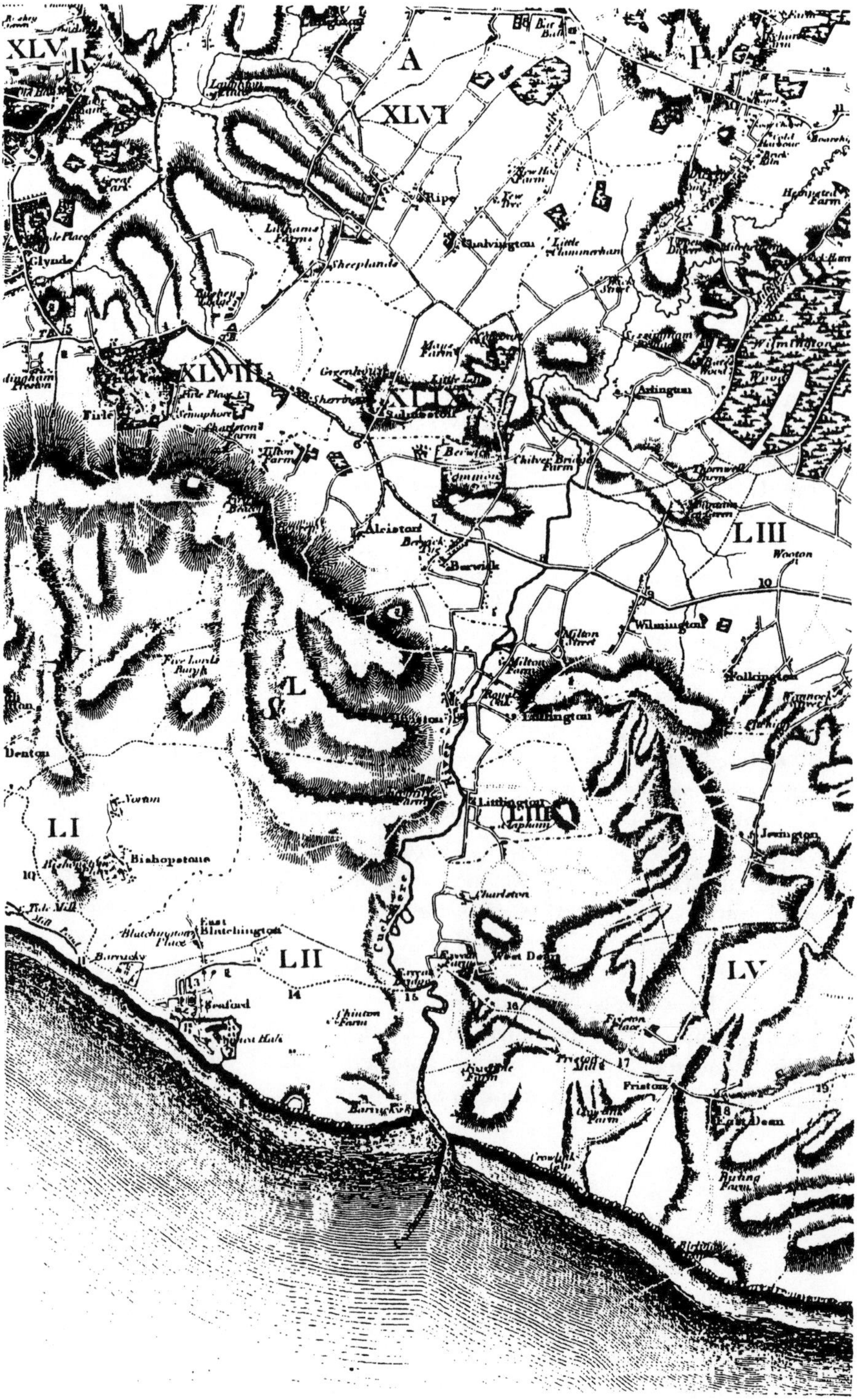

BACKCLOTH

In 1815 Britain at last emerged from the Napoleonic Wars. It was a remarkable achievement to have stuck to the task for so long and at such a cost, an estimated £625 million. And Britain was still the only major industrial country in the world, still the only serious exporter of manufactured goods. Yet, despite these advantages and this record of determination and skill, she managed in peacetime to experience a sustained economic depression which had many victims: small businessmen, artisans, industrial workers and, in particular, those employed in the largest of all industries, agriculture.

The farmworkers of Alfriston and the surrounding parishes - Berwick, Lullington, Litlington, Arlington - were inevitably affected by the economic decline. So too, to a greater or lesser extent, were the smaller farmers and skilled tradesmen and shopkeepers. When the major tenant farmers - at Frog Firle, Burnt House, Deans Place, Winton, Milton Court, Berwick Court, Lullington Court - had their rents raised, economies had to be practised but it was their labourers who bore the burden of slimmer regimes. As in all depressions some were more seriously affected than others: after 1815, the rich were perhaps less rich; the comfortable were possibly less comfortable; the poor were simply and abjectly poorer.

"Some of the villagers live like poor Irish peasants among their animals," Arthur Beckett wrote, describing what he had seen in Alfriston at the beginning of the present century. Eighty years before that life was even harder. Although there are no contemporary descriptions of how the poor lived in Alfriston, there were many witnesses over many years to give a clear enough picture of daily life. In 1821, the 107 dwellings in Alfriston, according to a document lent to Florence Pagden years later, housed 648 people. Cobbett in the 1820s saw "miserable dwellings" in the county and twelve year old Thomas Orton, a Sussex ploughboy, described his home to the Poor Law Commission in the early 1840s:

"We are 11 in all; there are five brothers and three sisters. We all sleep in one room except father and mother. There are three beds in one room and there are four rooms."

Others were to describe rural conditions as "brutal and wretched", the labourers' cottages "a scandal to England". James Fraser's report in 1867 offers further graphic substance to the picture which had not changed from earlier years.

"Modesty must be an unknown virtue, decency an unimaginable thing, where, in one small chamber, with the beds lying as thickly as they could be packed, father, mother, young men, lads grown and growing girls - two and sometimes three generations - are herded promiscuously; where every operation of the toilette and of nature - dressings, undressings, births, deaths - is performed by each within the sight or hearing of all; where children of both sexes, to as high an age as 12 or 14, or even more, occupy the same bed; where the whole atmosphere is sensual and human nature is degraded into something below the level of the swine."

It is against this background of chronic rural poverty that crime and disorder need to be considered.

Alfriston, with a population which had risen from 590 in 1811 to 648 in 1821 and to its peak of 694 by 1831, was the centre to which the surrounding parishes looked. The village - rather pompously it sometimes called itself 'the town' - had prospered from the wars. Brickmaking had flourished with the need to build military defences along the coast; the brewery had prospered from the influx of soldiers into the area; the leather industry had benefited in the wartime boom. None, however, prospered so much as the tenant farmers.

Thomas Geering, born early in the nineteenth century, never forgot the Alfriston of his childhood. The picture he paints may be over-enthusiastic but it is in keeping with what others have written and said about the place and the period. Writing of those palmy days, he tells of "the brewery with its vans and drays, sleek horses and burly faced draymen ... The two old inns were always full of company; volunteers and militiamen filled the place. Drinking, cursing and swearing went hand in hand." He describes a buzzing community where "the butcher did a large business and made money", where there were tanners, tawers, tallow melters, candlemakers, soapboilers, coopers and "shoemakers by the dozen".

He could have mentioned builders and carpenters, too, tailors and grocers, smiths and wheelwrights, all of whose businesses flourished. And there were glovemakers and saddlers, carriers and carters. He could have written about the farm lads coming down from Berwick, for where else could they buy their workboots? Or the farmers from Litlington visiting the saddler. It was to Alfriston that men from Arlington came for their corduroy working trousers and the girls and women for their dresses and stockings. And from tiny Lullington, that never numbered more than fifty souls, they came for practically everything. One has the impression that landless as he now was and with his condition deteriorating, even the poor labourer was still not as hopelessly impoverished as he was to be within the space of a few years.

On the narrow Cuckmere, Geering tells us, as though describing cargo from the Orient, "barges floated down ... and round to Newhaven, returning with merchandise of all sorts". Horsfield, less romantically inclined, states that the barges' principal cargoes were sea beach, seaweed and coals.

"The old town," Geering says, "was at the height of its glory but the hour of change and decay was at hand. The day of Waterloo sounded the knell to the prosperity of many a town on the Sussex coast besides Alfriston."

Geering, writing in the 1880s, continues his bleak account. In his lifetime he had observed the decay of his birthplace.

"Ultimately the brewery rotted to the ground and the vaults and cellars became a retreat for dogs and truant boys and girls to skulk in. There was no sale for such property. The brewers' occupation was gone, there being not enough money to pay for the beer and so what befell the brewhouse followed and swept away all the other principal trade buildings. The fine tannery became a desolation and the workmen drifted away into other occupations and other homes; and so it came about that the grocer, the shoemaker and another one or two minor callings are all that is left of the once flourishing trade of Alfriston."

Not all of these effects were experienced immediately after 1815. Indeed, some were not apparent for another twenty years and more, but the spiralling descent had set in quite soon after the war's end.

It was not just Alfriston and its satellite parishes, not solely towns on the coast of Sussex, which suffered a reversal in their fortunes. Across the country, men in every conceivable trade were crushed by a mighty new poverty. In Alfriston's small community the brickworks closed; the brewery lingered till the late 1830s but until then its path was downwards; the tannery did not close until 1843 but its fortunes, like those of many other rural tanyards, were in decline many years earlier. And all other trades felt the savage pinch.

The farmworkers suffered most. Long years before, their parents and grandparents had been driven from the land which the labour of generations had rendered fruitful. No longer sleeping under their masters' roofs, no more feeding at their masters' tables, they rented cheap accommodation in the village, paying for it and their food out of money wages. Now, post-war, they bore the brunt of economic fluxes, carried the weight of inflation, and were supported reluctantly, in these days of unemployment or under-employment, out of the local Poor Rate, paid for and administered by local men, farmers and tradesmen, who seemed not to share their distress and in some cases not to understand it. And when they could no longer pay their way, they would end up in houses owned and rented out to the Parish as poorhouses by such as Charles and William Brooker, leading members of the Parish Vestry, then the most powerful instrument of local government. Or they might find accommodation in the back quarters of Market Cross House let by the butcher, Stanton Collins, "to the Churchwardens and Overseers of the Poor of the Parish of Alfriston aforesaid and by them used as an Almshouse for the paupers belonging to the said Parish". How could paupers rise, restore their meagre fortunes? They could not. This was a sick and hopeless time.

And here was an interesting outcome of the war. Local men, ambitious tradesmen for the most part, had bought up property in those wartime years. The Hiltons, shoemakers, had bought houses; so too had the Brookers who, from a modest enough background, had broken into tanning and farming; James Collins, a butcher from Chiddingly, had purchased the huge and rambling Market Cross House in 1815; and Winch, the cooper, was another who had his own house as did members of the Bodle family. And several other families of quite humble beginnings had seen some prospects in property ownership. Backwater or no, Alfriston had produced some astute men of business. They had gone up in the world, raised themselves to new social heights. Some of the wealthier tenant farmers as well as the wretched labourers must at times have looked askance at such class-hopping, at so many they might regard as upstarts, enjoying such dramatically changed fortunes.

These men, "substantial house owners" all of them, along with farmers like Pagden and Dray and King, made up the Parish Vestry, fulfilling in their own time the functions of today's local and central government, with responsibilities for welfare, medical services, public order and local works. They set the Poor Rate and allocated it as and where necessary. They served voluntarily and unpaid as Churchwardens and Overseers of the Poor, as Constables, as Surveyors of Highways. They appointed as Parish Doctor Joseph Cooley who, for an annual fee of £10 plus additional payment for "labours, broken limbs and small pox", ministered to the poor. These Vestrymen, the Brookers, Marchants, Newmans, Woodhams and Hiltons and other tradesmen like Haryott the baker and Kidd the saddler, danced to no landed gentleman's tune. Here the gentry and the nobility remained at a distance though their tenants, the farmers, were always aware of their landlords' expectations and as Vestry members could be relied upon to bear these in mind. But on day-to-day matters it was these men, tradesmen and farmers, who made decisions which directly affected the lives of the poor.

In the background to Vestry members' decisions and labourers' woe was the clatter of national public disorder. There were the Swing Riots which spilt across the south in 1830 after the previous year's bad harvest, after the worst winter for ninety years. And with the fear of worse to come the labourers and small tradesmen demonstrated over three or four months. Their demonstrations, although involving great numbers, were most often conducted with dignity and good humour. There was only one death and that was of a man slain by a member of the Yeomanry. At the end, despite the moderate behaviour of the mobs, a frightened government tried nearly two thousand men, sent five hundred of them to Australia for terms of seven and fourteen years, and hanged nineteen.

There was yet more clamour over the introduction of the Parliamentary Reform Act of 1832 with serious riots in many towns and cities. There were disturbances in Horsham, Rye, Brighton and other Sussex towns, though the extension of the franchise was not really the business of any poor man. Only eighteen men in Alfriston would have the property qualifications which would enable them to vote in 1832. They would without exception vote in two Whigs, Messrs Curteis and Cavendish, scions of the landed class which, in spite of all its fears, had not let loose its grip on the lives of the majority of the population. For many others of Alfriston's 324 men and 324 women survival, not voting rights, was what mattered. Labourers had been better off in 1790 with wages at 6/- a week and beef only 2½d a lb, and tea, cheese, flour and candles cheap enough too. Thirty or so years later, with wages something in the order of 8/- to 10/-, such commodities represented a very much greater proportion of weekly earnings.

Poverty was the real problem. Yet there were solutions. The Reverend Thomas Robert Malthus had had the solution to both poverty and the poor. In his view, through their propensity to breed in unreasonably large numbers, the poor threatened food supplies. Where would it all end if unchecked? His proffered answer to the problem was to cut down on Parish Relief and allow the poor to starve. After all, they contributed nothing to the wealth of the nation. Indeed they took from it. Their survival did not matter.

Some of Malthus' propositions, promulgated in 1798, influenced the new Poor Law Act introduced in 1834. This was a serious attempt to resolve the problem of the poor and at the same time to reduce the rates. The solution was to make the poor work - regardless of the shortage of opportunities - or let them want. If they were in want, off to the new Workhouse with them - locally, Eastbourne for men and women, placed in separate wards; Seaford for their children. The aim was to make the system efficient, to make it cheap, to make it nasty. The old village poorhouses and the outdoor benefit system administered by the Vestry could no longer cope: the new system was intended to usher in a more effective way of resolving the problem.

Beyond resentment and fear of the Workhouse there was a sense of betrayal felt by many country folk. When local paths, used for generations, were closed against them by local farmers, such as Woodhams at Lullington; when they were prosecuted for the theft of a few apples or a faggot of wood valued at a penny by farmers like Ade; when they could not legally take a rabbit for the pot from Dray's land; when landowners and tenant farmers denied what ordinary countrymen had regarded as their natural rights, the rift was almost unbridgeable.

What could labouring men expect from a government or a master or a Vestry which treated them so? The period from 1815 until the 1870s was the most cruel ever for English agricultural workers. Shamefully treated, betrayed, bearing the burden of financial stringency, small wonder they were not always honest, that sometimes they were motivated by anger and revenge. The poor, it was thought, owed it to their superiors to be grateful and dutiful; it was thought they owed it to their betters to be thrifty, prudent, moral. Such expectations were too much for many. Crime and disorder and a growing disdain on the part of the poor towards those whom they believed had let them down, scarred the period.

UNUTTERABLY BANAL ... STULTIFYING ORDINARINESS

Do not expect Alfriston to provide evidence of much dramatic crime. Most offences were against property. There are few cases of violence against the person. There is one accusation of rape, some minor assaults, and several troublesome instances of damage committed, as we would say, by hooligans. That is the level at which most accusations would be pitched. In general, these people stole hens, scythes, sheep, jackets. Sometimes they broke into barns and stole peas or sacks of barley. For the most part, these were petty and desperately conducted offences.

Arson, of course, was a not irregular occurrence. And it was serious. Usually it seems to have been motivated out of a spirit of revenge against particular employers. Perhaps some had a political motivation: one may, for example, wonder if the Berwick Court fire of 1830 was in any way influenced by the Swing protest or if the fire at Frog Firle in 1834 would have occurred if the detested Poor Law Act had not been introduced.

There was some smuggling, too, though no cases involving Alfriston men came before the courts in the 1820s or 1830s. Stanton Collins, the butcher, whose local reputation rests upon an alleged career as a smuggler, had no smuggling charges brought against him in spite of what imaginative guide book writers have invented. Against that, it is inconceivable to think that Collins and other local men were not involved in this lucrative trade. This was large-scale, organised crime, very complex, involving significant numbers of people - hundreds of men on beaches, bringing goods ashore, loading pack animals and carts, escorting the wines and tobacco, lace and silks, to drop-off points higher up country. The distribution network itself gave employment to hundreds before the wine found itself in the MP's cellar, the tobacco in the great merchant's pipe, the spirits on the judge's table. In all of this vast hierarchy, it is not possible to say where or at what level Collins fitted in, or indeed the degree to which smuggling affected the lives of any individual persons in the area in the 1820s.

But most of the crime committed was of an unutterably banal nature, often of stultifying ordinariness. Take the following as a typical offence.

William Ford kept a public house just across the river from Alfriston. He described what occurred on 11th February 1835 in the following deposition which bears his mark, a quavery cross:

"I keep The Royal Oak Public House in Longbridge in the Parish of Lullington in this County. Yesterday evening the Prisoners Richard Lower and Stephen Lewis came into my House and called for a Pint of Beer. They afterwards had two Pints more and remained in the House till about quarter past nine. I had some Bacon Hams in my Kitchen Chimney. In the course of the day as I sat by the fire I noticed that the Hams were in the Chimney two or three times. There were three Hams there at those times. I noticed that the prisoner Lower appeared to be watching me about the House which made me suspicious of him. The other prisoner Stephen Lewis gave me a little Pook [poke] and pointed up the Chimney. I called my wife to wait in the Kitchen and went out at the Back Door and sent my next door Neighbour Mrs. Burfield for Edward Reeds who lives close by. I returned immediately to the Kitchen and the Prisoner went out of the House almost directly. I then looked up the Chimney with a Candle. I discovered that one Ham of the three was gone. I asked my daughter who had come in from the Bar into the Kitchen whether she had taken one of the Hams down. She said 'No'. I am not certain whether I asked my wife the same question or whether she was in the Kitchen or at the Bar Door when I asked my daughter. I then went out of doors and I saw the Prisoner come back into the House. I went up to the Prisoner Lower and asked him what he had done with the Ham. He said he did not know anything about it. I told him I was certain he did know. He said if I would let him go he would tell me where it was. I told him I should not let him go till somebody else came. He said he would go and fetch it. I told him he should go in a-doors and I led him in a-doors. He still wanted to go after the Bacon but I told him I would not let him go till somebody else came. James Cox a neighbour soon came in. I asked Cox to take the Man to go with him after the Bacon. In three or four Minutes they came back with Edward Reeds, who had the Bacon in his Hand. I saw the Ham and was sure it was my Ham. All that Lower said and did was quite voluntary. I sent for the Constable, Richard Hilton, and delivered the Prisoner to him."

Lower, a 33 year old baker, seems to have been remarkably inept as a thief. On the other hand, he is alleged to have told Hilton that he stole the ham in order to be caught and sent to prison. If so, his wish was granted. He was given two months' hard labour. His companion, Lewis, was discharged.
Why would a man wish to go to prison? Are we to believe that he sincerely wished for this? After all, he offered to return the ham from where he had hidden it in the hedge by the roadside. After the commission of the offence did he change his mind? Did he perhaps hope to avoid the rigours of winter in the belief that a prison cell would be preferable to whatever accommodation he now had? Or was he in so low a state that it was a case of prison or Eastbourne Workhouse? It is difficult to assess motives across such a stretch of time and in the absence of other revealing documentation. But Lower was a baker. Was there no work for him even after the bumper harvest of 1834? Or was he as poor a baker as he was inept a thief?
As to Ford, what persuaded him to summon his neighbours? Certainly, many minor offences were resolved privately without recourse to the law. Perhaps he just felt it was the right thing to do. Or was he trying to prove himself a worthy, law-abiding citizen? He and members of his family were members of Alfriston's Independent Chapel. There had been earlier complaints of bad conduct at The Royal Oak and only the year before, Charles Brooker, senior trustee of the chapel, and another chapel committee man, James Awcock, a shoemaker, had been deputed to talk to Ford about lack of order. Happily, they had been able to report back that they were confident that the Fords would "do all they can

to discontinue vice and keep good order in the House".

Vice?

Certainly nothing on any grand scale comes to mind. Ford's licence would have been withdrawn had there been anything which hinted at serious matters. There was drunkenness, most likely. Excess drinking was endemic in rural areas and there is no reason to suspect that The Royal Oak was any different from many other public houses. Swearing, too. Geering mentioned that as common. But the strait-laced chapel community of Alfriston would certainly disapprove of that. Perhaps that was the offence that took Brooker and Awcock there. Or possibly there were matters of snared rabbits; nudges and winks about some kindling in the hedgerow. Certainly Ford seems not the kind of man to encourage blatant dishonesty unlike William Adams of The George who some years earlier had lost his licence. In fact, Ford would maintain his good name until 1838 when, as the Chapel Minute Book records, he "Died in the Lord".

The constable, Richard Hilton, who was called to The Royal Oak, had been elected to the office by the Parish Vestry of which he was a member. He was obliged to carry out his unpaid duties for a twelvemonth and then he might hope that someone else might take on the task. But he was young, only in his thirties, and maintaining the law was not old man's work. At times it was both tiresome and dangerous. In this feeble way, through such frail instruments, law in the countryside was inefficiently maintained. Nor would many English people have it any other way: the French might have a full-time, paid police force but here such a body was considered an affront to liberty, a prop to tyranny.

In 1830, Peel received a printed placard threatening his new metropolitan force in somewhat feverish terms. How aptly it illustrates the attitude of some sections of the population.

"PEEL'S POLICE RAW LOBSTERS BLUE DEVILS
or by whatever other appropriate name they may be known:-
Notice is hereby given of subscription to arm the people with STAVES of a superior Effect (against) a Force unknown to the British Constitution."

It was the last point, that a police force was alien to the Constitution, that many not unreasonable men and women subscribed to.

Only in 1840 did Alfriston receive its first policeman - Constable N° 6, Robert Baker. His role was profoundly different from that of Richard Hilton who, like his predecessors, made arrests, escorted vagrants from the parish and accompanied accused parties to court. But the pursuit of offenders and their prosecution was most usually the responsibility of the victim. For example, William Haylor, whose ass was stolen from Alfriston in the 1830s, traced the culprit, Samuel Barnes, a 41 year old labourer, to Poynings. Haylor was then responsible for taking the case to court. As a result, Barnes was sentenced to eight months' imprisonment, the first two and last two months in solitary confinement.

During the troubles of the 1830s matters were so bad what with ricks being fired, sheep stolen or maimed, barns broken into, that night-time patrols were introduced, paid for by farmers and tradesmen but there is no evidence of their having caught anyone. Perhaps they served as a deterrent.

One institution was designed principally to prevent arson, theft, damage to property, sheep rustling and maiming. For much of the century the Alfriston Society for Prosecuting Felons and Thieves, to which most landowners and farmers belonged, had been established. It existed largely to offer mutual support and rewards for information about specific offences. Although precise details of the Alfriston Society are not now available, they would be similar to that at Ticehurst. There, members paid 2/- every six months until a balance of £50 was reached. Subscriptions then stopped until the pool was reduced to £30 when the sum would be topped up. When any member was robbed or defrauded he would give notice to the Society's clerk who would decide on whether or not an offender, if known, should be prosecuted. Funds would be expended on prosecution costs and rewards would be offered to informants who might expect to receive up to £5 for information leading to the successful prosecution of arsonists, stealers of sheep or corn, and £2 for cases involving the theft of fruit, fowl or wood. Despite such rewards few were ever claimed.

The commission of crime, then, was scarcely restrained by

constables, patrols or the Prosecuting Society. One of the greatest encouragements to crime as the magistrate, John Fielding, had observed in the previous century, was the probability that the perpetrators would so often go undetected. With such a low detection rate there is no way of knowing the numbers of crimes committed in this period: no records have been found and it is likely that few were kept. Newspaper reporting was also spasmodic.

There were patterns, however, of crime and criminals. Richard Burnett, the chaplain of Lewes Gaol, maintained regular records of prisoners and their offences. Writing about the convicts, many of whom were young, he said that, "the great majority are of those that earn a precarious livelihood by labouring work, having no certain employment of any kind, especially in winter". Of 333 prisoners in 1838-1839, 290 were male. Of these 206 were labourers. Of the remainder, fifteen were shoemakers, seven were errand boys. There were few representatives of any other skilled trades. 60 had been found guilty of the theft of corn, fowl and wood, and 124 had taken small items from houses and shops. Most in the latter category came from larger towns committing their offences in places such as Brighton. There were fifteen sheep stealers and three horse thieves, convicted of crimes which until very recently had carried the death penalty.

Burnett attributed crime to extreme poverty, lack of education and excessive drinking as well as severe unemployment. It was his opinion that transportation, which in the 1830s reached its peak, was no deterrent. Many were said to have regarded it as a chance to start a new life and Burnett mentions a book, circulating among the prisoners, extolling life in Australia and the opportunities it offered once a man's time as a convict was spent. In Burnett's view two years' hard labour was a more effective deterrent. Poor food, grim accommodation and a regular turn on the treadmill, in the chaplain's view, represented a better use of taxpayers' money.

So in the villages and in the prisons too, were large numbers of young men, a huge dispossessed group, landless, hungry, and with few of the loyalties to the old order that their fathers and grandfathers are alleged to have possessed.

Whose fault? A harsh, unfeeling government some would say. And an out-of-touch landowning class they might add. According to others it was attributable to grasping, mean-spirited tenant farmers. Or it might have been the sheer force of numbers, including 250,000 demobilised soldiers, returned from the Peninsula or America or India, providing more recruits for an already swollen labour market. All such factors might have been responsible for a severe deterioration in the living standards of the families of labouring men.

The landowning classes were undeniably often out of touch. If Marie Antoinette did not really recommend cake, the Duke of Norfolk made up for her. His advice was that the hungry poor should lay in a stock of curry powder.

> "A pinch of this powder," he advised, "mixed with warm water ..... warms the stomach incredibly .... and a man without food can go to bed comfortably on it."

Nor in all the tribulations of the period do those living in Alfriston and the surrounding parishes hear much from the aristocratic landowners to encourage them. Lord Gage at Firle is relatively silent; we hear nothing from the Burlingtons; General Chowne is mute. Nor does Countess Amherst contribute much. She lets out her 871 acres in tiny Lullington to the Woodhams family who have farmed there for generations. But her presence is not felt. From the Earl of Plymouth there is some reaction only when his tenant's barns at Milton Court are burnt out.

And the larger tenant farmers, though their profits diminished after the war, nevertheless enjoyed improved living standards at the cost of tightening their labourers' belts. Wages were lower; less work was offered; tools lasted longer; carts were less frequently repaired; bills were paid less promptly. That was how the tenant farmers more than survived.

And what of those traditional rights taken from the landless? How did the young Alfriston butcher, William Pearson, admittedly an acknowledged criminal, feel about his fine for snaring rabbits at Deans Place? And did Henry Page, a labourer, living in Chapple Houses, Lullington, believe himself to be a criminal when in 1837 he received one week's imprisonment for the theft of "one faggot to the value of one penny"?

Admittedly there was a problem which no great lord, no Vestry member, no cleric nor tenant farmer could resolve. Government at parish level - the Vestry - faced a massive explosion of population in a period when agriculture, the main industry, had begun to need fewer workers. The figures are frightening. More and more was being paid out in rates to feed the poor, yet their standards of living were continually in decline. In 1751 the population of Britain has been assessed at six million. Fifty years on, the population had risen to ten million. By 1841, there were eighteen million inhabitants in these islands. As for Sussex the population rose from 160,000 in 1801 to 300,000 in 1841. As the population had climbed so steeply in so short a time, there was a huge surplus of young men available for work. More and more money in rates was needed to pay for these young unemployed men. It was the consequences of these facts and figures which the governments, central and local, were obliged to face.

In a time of declining work opportunities when it was the young who failed to find work, fathers with at least three children were favoured by employers. They were paid low wages which the Vestry made up to about 10/-. The farmers, as the largest employers, benefited most from these arrangements, the Poor Rate being used as a form of subsidy for inadequate wages. Young single men qualified for lower benefits. Even so, there were enough critics to say the young were idle and dissolute, content to live on handouts. A Poor Law Report of 1834 quotes a Jevington farm labourer, Thomas Pearce, who thinks little of those of his fellows whose money comes from the Parish and who in turn are expected to do some work in return, either on farms or roads. It seems they need better supervision.

"They get the same money and don't do half so much work. They don't work like me. They be'ant at it so many hours and they don't do so much work when they be at it. They're doing no good and are only waiting for dinner time and night. They be'ant working. It's only waiting."

Thomas Geering was of the opinion that the labourers themselves were to blame for their plight.

"Men in the full vigour of life," he wrote, "did not hesitate to throw themselves on the Parish. Relief in money or in Kind, or both, could not be refused. Self-help was not understood among our labouring population, neither was the glorious privilege of being independent recognised: we were in an abyss of degradation and moral degeneracy."

But how could the rural labourer elevate himself, improve his position, when he rarely received enough to support himself and his family without applying to the Parish? Under this system a man could not fall too far: he would be borne up by parish relief. Yet he could not rise too high: his meagre wages ensured that. Thus, the incentive to work, the ability to make himself independent and to relish the privilege was denied him. His hope, ambition and chances of improving his life were stifled.

Some families, desperate, sought work in other parishes. But once their employment came to an end, they were unceremoniously hustled back to their parish of origin under the 1824 Vagrancy Act, which had been placed on the Statute Book to resolve the serious problems of the huge and expanding number of vagrants at large. In 1827, a year in which many Vagrancy Orders were put before Sussex magistrates, Richard Wilson, a labourer, with his wife, Elizabeth, and Frances Wilson, a single woman presumably related to them, were sent back to Alfriston from the Lewes parish of St John under the Castle. It must be assumed that they had moved there from Alfriston either with the promise of work which had ended or with the intention of begging at the more populous place. Some years later Wilson's son, a bricklayer living in the High Street, would have his parents under his roof rather than send them to the Workhouse.

This was a period of steeply rising crime. Some of its causes were social and economic. It may be argued that the contribution of the landed classes and tenant farmers was less than praiseworthy. In mitigation, it is undeniable that the problems posed by a rising population and increasingly limited opportunities of employment were not easily capable of resolution by those in power.

SOME CRIMES : 1822 - 1825

1822

Henry Spurgeon, a labourer, stole a cotton shirt valued at one shilling, belonging to Charles Reeds. He was fined one shilling and sentenced to one year's hard labour.

1824

Henry Pagden of Frog Firle complained that he, like other farmers, had "for some Time past lost divers Quantities of Oats, Barley and Peas".

A press report claimed that the district was infested with "plunderers" who stole clothing, tools and anything edible from farms. Pagden's men lost jackets and lunch boxes.

Copper piping was stolen from Alfriston Church and in Folkington a large copper sundial was taken by thieves.

1825

Henry West stole a scythe (7/6) belonging to Henry Hilton and another valued at 6/- belonging to John Westgate. He was transported for seven years.

THE ALFRISTON DISORDERS : 1825 - 1828

There is a sense in which the most interesting offences of the mid-1820s were those which occurred in the centre of Alfriston and which had their origins in the hatred which had developed between two of its most influential men, Charles Brooker and Stanton Collins. The disturbances which grew out of their animosity gave the opportunity to boys and young men of the village to demonstrate against the Parish Officers.

Overseers of the Poor, senior members of the Vestry, had a frequently difficult role to fulfil. When claimants applied for relief, Overseers were required to assess their degree of need and were therefore obliged to put questions about any wages the claimant might be earning; about other wage earners in the family; about the number of children; about the general health of the family. This information was then presented to the Vestry who would determine whether or not to give relief. The questions were sometimes resented, regarded as intrusive, and those who asked them were in consequence often unpopular. A crude kind of means test was in operation throughout the country with some Overseers and Vestries easier on benefit claimants than others. Edward Ellman, Vicar of Berwick, accused Alfriston Vestry of over-generosity but such judgements are often imprecise.

The first incident in the campaign against Alfriston's Parish Officers was reported in the Sussex Advertiser of 12th December 1825.

"On the night of 4th or 5th inst., some evil-minded person or persons maliciously cut down and destroyed upwards of one hundred choice apple and pear trees growing in the orchard of Mr. William Brooker of Alfriston. The night being extremely dark, it is supposed the villains must have been well acquainted with the ground."

This act heralded a year-long series of mischievous attacks on the property of the Parish Officers, particularly that of William

Brooker, the Churchwarden, his brother Charles, the Overseer of the Poor, John Newman, also an Overseer, and Richard Hilton whose particular office at that time is unknown.

The damage to the orchard might be seen as a hugely symbolic act. At that time it was customary in winter for a night-time ceremony - in Sussex called 'apple yowling' - to be held in local orchards. Parties of labourers would conduct a ceremony redolent of pagan magic, sprinkling one of the trees with cider or hanging cakes soaked in cider from the branches. The men, joining hands, would dance and sing around the tree after which they would be invited into their masters' houses to drink and eat.

At Selmeston, not half a dozen miles from Alfriston, the song ran:

> "Here's to thee, old apple tree
> Mays't thou bud, mays't thou blow,
> Mays't thou bear apples enow."

What happened to William Brooker's orchard seems a savage parody of the old ceremonial. It was an act of spite against a man who for many years had carried out a variety of duties as a Parish Officer. Now, as Churchwarden, he was being blamed, as often members of the Vestry were, for the low level of parish relief. As in many other instances it required little for him to become a target of the discontented poor.

What, however, on this occasion had stirred so much anger was not simply the level of poor relief but unrelated charges against Stanton Collins and William Adams brought before the magistrates by or at least at the instigation of the Parish Officers. Resentful that these two men - Collins the butcher and Adams, landlord of The George - had been unfairly singled out, "many determined young men were heard to vent the most violent threats".

Adams had been accused of permitting "tippling and drunkenness in his [public] house", and a prosecution against him was instigated by the Parish Officers and by Ministers of the chapel and several prominent inhabitants. Alfriston had a strong non-conformist tradition which frowned on the excesses in public houses and beershops. In this, it shared the widespread concerns about rural drunkenness at that time. Collins and his coterie met at The George and it was these who especially resented the prosecution of Adams. That the wealthy Collins, who might have been expected to mix with the more respectable and comfortable citizenry, preferred to consort with the poor, heavy-drinking labourers must have puzzled and enraged his more upright contemporaries. It was among this group, of course, that he recruited those who would fall in with his criminal projects.

At the same time as the charge against Adams was brought forward, a charge of rape had been preferred against Collins. Earlier in the year the Vestry had arranged for Jemima Coot, a young pauper, to work for Collins in return for her board and keep. She left Collins' house abruptly and complained to the Parish Officers that she had been raped by her master and stated that she would prefer to be sent to prison rather than stay at Market Cross House. She was taken to the village Workhouse where both the Master and his wife believed her account of what had occurred. The Parish Officers then persuaded Jemima to prosecute Collins who was charged and ordered to appear before the Hailsham Magistrates in December 1825.

For lack of evidence the complaint against Collins was not proceeded with but the Magistrates were nevertheless sympathetic to the girl and to the Parish Officers who had urged her to bring her case before them. Collins was asked by the Magistrates to make some financial recompense to Jemima Coot, even though the case had made no headway. There is, however, no indication that Collins paid her anything. The likelihood is that in view of his continued protestations of innocence, he did not.

Before the same bench, Adams was fined £5 for abusing his licence. In the following year, he was to lose the licence and be imprisoned for twelve months for similar offences.

It was these cases of December 1825 which provoked the young men to stand up for Collins and Adams. It is of course strongly probable that Collins, an able and resolute man, encouraged them in what they did. Indeed, the depredations ought really to be seen as a serious personal struggle, a confrontation between Collins and the Parish Officers, particularly Charles Brooker.

It is perhaps bizarre but Collins was himself, by virtue of his wealth and property, classed as a "substantial householder" and therefore was a member of the Vestry which he attended regularly between 1820 and 1825. Unfortunately, there is no evidence of his attendance after that date as the relevant Vestry Minute Book is missing.

When the rivalry between Brooker and Collins really began it is impossible to say. Collins had been at Market Cross House since his father bought it in 1815. By 1825, Collins, then thirty, had purchased the house from his father and was taking his butchery trade seriously enough to build a slaughter house at the back of the property. By then, he ought to have earned a reputation as a solid member of the community by virtue of his large house and his capital but it must already have been apparent to many that he was not the responsible citizen he ought to have been. Presumably he was already involved in the smuggling he has always been associated with. Whilst some have called smugglers honest thieves and have suggested that what they did was not real crime, there were violent clashes and deaths in the 1820s and 1830s when men of the Preventive Service and smugglers met. Not everyone would treat smuggling so lightly: some in the chapel would not regard it with such indulgence.

But it was the other large-scale criminal activities in which Collins was involved - his theft of sheep and his breaking into barns - which would meet with the most severe disapproval among those who believed in the importance and sanctity of property. By 1825 doubts of his honesty were probably very firm and when the case against him went before the magistrates there might have been some satisfaction in the minds of those who had urged Jemima Coot to pursue her case.

One wonders too if any of the sober tradesmen of Alfriston had any idea that in 1824 Collins had fathered an illegitimate child and if so, how his reputation stood in this particular. When Maria Geering, a respectable dressmaker, had her daughter, Augusta, baptised, the name of the father was omitted from the Baptismal Register. Against the child's name are the words "…. base born - no father recorded". Twenty years later when Augusta Geering married, the Register shows Collins to be her father. Was this a secret all those years? Or merely an open secret?

No matter. Even if the facts of Augusta Geering's birth remained hidden, by 1825 her father's way of life must have been in strong contrast to that of most other tradesmen in the village. Many indeed must have felt let down by one who was of their social status, a Vestry member, conducting himself in such dubious ways, not merely libidinous if the story of rape was to be believed but also criminal. Collins, at this time, must have been regarded as a dangerous opponent of the established order, one who supported young men in their offences, who enlisted their help in his dishonest practices, who promoted criminality on a considerable scale. That Collins was sheep-stealing and barn-raiding, taking the property of respectable men in the locality, was most likely well-known though at this time inadequate proof existed of his offences.

In the last days of 1825 and through the following months a series of minor acts of vandalism took place at night. At the end of January, the Sussex Advertiser printed the following notice:

> "The Alfriston Annoyance-Mongers, who like Imps of Darkness embrace in the pursuit of their nefarious practices the dead of night, should now beware, lest they are dragged forth to the exposure of day, as it will be seen, by an advertisement in the preceding page, that a Reward of Ten Guineas is offered for their discovery and conviction."

Five guineas of this reward came from the Alfriston Prosecuting Society and five from the injured parties, the two Brookers and John Newman.

Charles Brooker's windows had been smashed on the preceding Saturday and the following night his brother William's garden gate was wrenched off and taken away and four panes of his parlour window were broken. John Newman's garden gates were also forced off their hinges and the gate posts uprooted.

> "It is frequently the practice of Drunken Parties breaking up about midnight," the Advertiser remarks, "to carry off garden gates and commit other mischievous acts to

the great annoyance and injury of the peaceable inhabitants."

No great imagination is required to guess where at this time the "Drunken Parties" had been taking place until midnight. William Adams had been fined: he had not yet lost his licence and his liberty.

The Advertiser opines that "the Constables ought surely to be on the alert to bring to justice these nightly depredations".

Truth to tell, the constables were often much too wise to entertain ideas of interrupting the boisterous behaviour of lusty farm lads in drink. And, furthermore, the constables were working men. They could not reasonably be expected to patrol the streets and lanes night after night. Some years later when a regular patrol was instituted even it had no perceptible success.

Charles Brooker's house was again singled out for attack on 1st March. Sitting with his wife at midnight, he heard the clatter of two horses outside. Then the windows were shattered a second time.

These disturbances were accompanied by a fascinating newspaper correspondence contributed by the principal participants. Charles Brooker was the first to take up his pen, his letter appearing in the Sussex Advertiser on 13th February. Addressing himself to the editor, he claimed that as a consequence of the cases involving Jemima Coot and William Adams, he had had his windows broken.

> "Still," he writes, "from the various facts in my possession, I am fully persuaded that the parish officers would have been extremely deficient in their duty, had they not on such an occasion, come forward in defence of a poor, unprotected and now orphan female, one of their paupers."

Brooker does not mention Collins by name in his letter. He merely hopes that the wrongdoer will repent and warns him: "Be sure your sins will find you out".

The following week, in a letter too good to pass over, Collins replied. His letter is addressed directly "To Charles Brooker,

Licensed Dealer in Pepper, Vinegar, Snuff, etc", as sneering an introduction as he can manage, reminding his enemy, in case he has social ambitions, that he is just a common tradesman. He goes on to accuse Brooker of "insatiable malice and revenge" and claims that the girl's character is not as Brooker and the Parish Officers have claimed. "I can prove by respectable witnesses that her veracity is not to be relied on."

Collins then with a freedom of expression which would be denied him today - perhaps sadly, for the innocent reader is robbed of some harmless entertainment - explodes. "You doltish and scurrilous Scribbler! I disclaim any such conduct and defy the whole world to prove that I was in any way implicated or accessory to it."

Next follows some further personal abuse, perhaps the most delightful of the whole correspondence. Suggesting that Brooker has climbed above his natural station, and dismissing him as if he alone were a village tradesman, Collins tells him to attend to his "pepper, vinegar, snuff and tobacco business".

Then Collins reverts for a moment to John Newman, Overseer of the Poor, partner of Brooker in the tannery and brother of Brooker's first wife Elizabeth. "I am not a stranger to his grinning grimaces nor his insignificance," Collins says. Then he turns to another target, to "the other active parish officer, your brother, old Billy Brooker ..... Do you not consider him immaculate enough to cast the first stone? .... or does he, coddling, kind hearted soul, in sympathy forbear?" And we wonder what piece of village gossip lies behind that statement.

But then it is back to the real enemy. Neither he nor his wife is spared:

> "When we reflect, Charles Brooker, that you are not a boy, but a man of 48, with five children, and recently married to a girl of 21, you should have displayed other feelings for my failings, and not use every exertion in your power to increase the distress and misery of my family and friends."

And next comes more small town snobbery and venomous scorn.

In his letter Brooker had written about his parlour windows. Parlour? Collins sneers.

"When we reflect how lately your father was a little, penny shaving, country barber in this place, if there had not been some profit in your pepper and vinegar career, and better friendship than you dispense to me, you might, I believe, have said kitchen, scullery, or any other window. You might as well have said drawing room window when you was about it."

Odd to think that these two men lived only forty yards or so apart.

John Newman took his turn to leap into print on 27th February. His long letter addressed to "Mr. Collins, Alfriston" is calm and reasoned. He claims never to have been unfriendly towards Collins in the past. On the contrary, he has offered him warnings about his behaviour "in the friendliest manner possible".

This is the sole hint up to now that perhaps Collins' behaviour has been either illegal or at least not in keeping with that expected of a respectable tradesman.

Newman, however, is unable to resist taking a swing at Collins, who cannot, he says, have written the letter in the previous week's edition. Newman claims to know Collins' linguistic skills well enough. Collins "has not the ability to write and spell in his own tongue".

Perhaps not.

But why, Newman asks, single out just three parish officers to attack? Others have regarded Collins as guilty.

"I suppose," Newman writes - and this is significant for it offers some evidence that the disagreements with Collins go back for some considerable time - "it is because we have forborne to have any dealings with you in trade".

And one wonders why - was it their disapproval of a man known beyond any doubt to be dishonest?

Collins is back into print on 6th March, claiming full responsibility for the confrontation of his earlier letter. As for Newman, he writes, "I consider your letter an unchristianlike,

35

ungentlemanly and unmanly production, worthy of yourself". But he can offer no further defence.

Here the correspondence ended and no other acts of damage were mentioned in the press for a while although a total peace was unlikely. Perhaps several minor acts of vandalism went unreported as they were no longer considered newsworthy.

In September garden robbers were said to be "audaciously active in Alfriston". Richard Hilton, the shoemaker, who some years later as Constable was to arrest Richard Lower at The Royal Oak, had his plum tree stripped of its fruit and the tree "much injured". Eight gallons of fruit were taken from William Woodhams' garden while Charles Brooker was once more a victim. This time his vine was robbed of fifty pounds of "fine, ripe grapes".

These crimes were not of the highest order but they do illustrate very well the dislike which some men entertained for Parish Officers and how they took opportunities to humiliate those seen as representatives of the law. It is, too, difficult not to see these personal attacks on the Officers as part of a vendetta orchestrated by Collins against those whom he claimed had wronged him by encouraging Jemima Coot to proceed against him and by punishing his friend Adams. Indeed, they seem to suggest the power which Collins exerted over a certain group of aggressive young men and boys.

The next recorded act of disorder is a curious enough affair, interesting only in that the principal victims were Charles Brooker and his family and that among the participants were two of Collins' followers, Samuel Thorncraft and Lewis Awcock, of whom more was to be heard later.

On the night of 6th November 1828 there occurred outside Brooker's house what was described as a riot. Thorncraft, Awcock, John Adams, all labourers, and Richard Wilson, a bricklayer, "with divers other evil disposed persons ... did assemble and meet together to disturb the peace of our Lord the King and then and there being so unlawfully and tumultuously assembled and gathered together and did then and there unlawfully riotously routously tumultuously violently and outrageously make a great noise riot tumult and disturbance".

The disturbance lasted up to six hours during which time the mob - though that seems too strong a term - collected piles of wood and set them alight. The fire which was very close to Brooker's house "greatly terrified the said Charles Brooker and his family".

At the Epiphany Sessions in 1829, Thorncraft was sentenced to one month's hard labour, Adams and Awcock to three weeks'. Richard Wilson was discharged.

What are we to make of this? Was the date significant? Had these youths, none of them yet twenty years of age, been to Lewes bonfire celebrations the night before? Had this excited them? Given them ideas? Had the notion of an Alfriston version of bonfire celebrations appealed to them? But why outside Brooker's house? Possibly because it was in the Square, the central place, the most obvious location for a bit of fun. But why taunt the most influential man in the village? Why taunt a man widowed for a second time only a year earlier when his twenty-three year old wife died? After all, he would recognise these youths, would know them all, would be in a position to charge them later. Was it worth it in the eyes of the young men to go to gaol for the satisfaction of annoying a parish official? Even one so influential as Brooker? And what of Collins? Was he behind any of this? Perhaps from his window he enjoyed the spectacle for Brooker's house was only forty yards away on the other side of the square.

And does this serve as a reminder of the unbroken thread of mindless hooliganism of young men and boys which has always run through English social life at all levels - mediaeval apprentices, Elizabethan gallants, London's eighteenth century mohocks, our own century's yobbish tendency? Were these lads simply demonstrating their disregard for law, order and respectability in the same way that in London, young bucks, wealthy and exclusive, were creating their own versions of public mayhem?

But then, it all seems rather small stuff in the scale of recorded criminal behaviour, a few broken windows, gates damaged, fruit stolen and some horseplay getting out of hand on an early winter evening. Even so, slight though it was, the law was demonstrably unable to contain it. For where was the constable on any of these occasions? Quite evidently a small, amateur constabulary could not easily fulfil the expectations of law-abiding men and women in the face of feckless disorder.

SOME CRIMES : 1826 - 1828

1826

John Potter and Thomas Twigg, labourers from South Malling, received a year's hard labour for stealing oats from Farmer Ridge's barn in Alfriston.

An accomplice, Stephen Gower, was not charged after he offered evidence against the others.

Samuel Thorncraft, a seventeen year old, was sentenced to one month's hard labour for the theft of seven apples from his employer, Charles Ade of Milton Court Farm.

1827

Charles Brooker's shop was a target of shoplifters. Henry Walker, labourer, was sentenced to two months' hard labour for stealing 2lb of bacon (1/-).

William Kemp, labourer, was found not guilty by the same court of stealing 1lb of bacon (6d).

Anne Bowling, a servant of Walter Woodhams of Lullington Court Farm, was accused of pretending to Brooker's shop assistant that her mistress wanted ½lb of mustard and six oranges. In a confusing case, she was found not guilty of trying to obtain goods by false pretences.

1828

Thomas Reed, a sixty year old farm worker, was found guilty of stealing two oaken poles (1/-) and three pieces of elm board (1/-) from Lord Gage's land.

He was sentenced to fourteen days' solitary confinement.

SOME CASES OF ARSON : 1822 - 1831

From the 1790s there had been an increase in the county of outbreaks of arson, both major and minor. Sometimes small ricks went up in flames: at other times whole barns were consumed. Whilst tools, wagon and machine breaking had always been a method by which disgruntled workers had avenged themselves for real or imagined grievances, such damage did not have such far-reaching consequences as arson.

The increases in insurance premiums paid to Sun Fire and The Norwich, two of the principal institutions, were alarming to farmers cutting back on costs. For their part, the insurance companies were obliged to ask their agents to enquire locally about how well a farmer was liked before agreeing premiums.

But it was the scale of the outbreaks which developed in these early decades of the century which was the source of anxiety beyond the immediate farming community. Mrs Ann Marchant, wife of the Alfriston saddler, wrote in January 1832: "We were dreadfully alarmed with the fires and have no doubt but the greater part of Alfriston would have been consumed before the winter had ended." Of course private houses were very rarely attacked by arsonists and no such cases occurred in Alfriston, but Mrs Marchant was nevertheless exhibiting a very real fear which many shared.

There was something alien about arson. It had been relatively rare in England - representing only 1% of crimes - and it was generally regarded as a foreign import, something from revolutionary France, so that the fires which flared up now seemed to hint at dark things, anarchy, revolution. After all, there was something deeply irrational about a crime by which men robbed themselves of winter threshing which represented up to twelve weeks' work. Arson was inexplicable, extreme and frightening.

In 1822 incendiarism reached one of its peaks. The following is an account of the fire at Folkington. The victim, farmer Stephen Searle, was a subscriber to the Alfriston Prosecuting Society.

"Examination of Stephen Searle of the Parish of Folkington within the Hundred of Longbridge in the County of Sussex Yeoman taken on Oath the first Day of April in the Year of our Lord one thousand eight hundred and twenty two .....

.... about ten o'clock in the night of Thursday the twenty eighth Day of March now last past a Fire broke out in some Ricks in a Close adjoining his Dwelling House ... which continued burning during the whole of the Night and until the following Morning - that consumed one Stack of Wheat one stack of Beans and one Rick of Oats ... Also a Barn occupied by this Examinant containing between eight and nine Loads of unthreshed Wheat and a Threshing Machine therein ... Also a granary ... and upwards of thirty Quarters of Oats three Sacks of Beans three Sacks of Wheat about five hundred Oil Cakes, two Quarters of Clover Seeds, about twenty one Dozen of Brooms about a Sack of Malt, about fifty empty Sacks, a Malt Mill, two Sacks Waggons and a Considerable Quantity of Corn and Hay Rakes, Scuppits, Bushel Measures, Shalls, Sieves, Hay and Corn Forks ... Dung Cart ... about eight Wattles and two Pig Troughs ... and this Examinant saith that the said Stacks and other premises were wilfully and maliciously set on fire by some person or persons at present unknown ... the whole value of the property so consumed amounts at least to the Sum of five hundred Pounds."

On the other side of the page is a letter from the Solicitors, Messrs King and Gell of Lewes, which says:

"In addition to the Circumstances stated by Mr. Searle, Mr. Pagden of Folkington who first saw the Fire says that he observed three separate Fires burst forth nearly at the same Moment from three Stacks, each Fire seemingly rising from the Bottom of the Stack on the Leeward side and consequently not having been communicated from the one to the other, but having been separately set on fire."

A second letter from the solicitors to the MP, Edward Curteis, says that the Alfriston Prosecuting Society was offering a reward of £50. It continues:

"Mr. Searles's Property was unfortunately not insured; but the Buildings which were burnt had been insured by Mr. William Harison the Landlord in the Sun Fire Office. There is no Doubt that the Office will likewise offer a Reward."

Whether the Sun did or did not offer a reward, is not known. No culprit was ever discovered.

During the summer and autumn of 1830 the Swing Riots spread across the eastern and southern English counties. After the worst winter in ninety years and prospects of a second successive bad harvest, farm labourers demonstrated in large numbers for better wages, more generous relief and the abandonment by farmers of threshing machines. Incendiarism was marginal in Sussex. There were only twenty or so outbreaks of fire including those at East Dean and at Court Farm, Berwick. There were of course disorders in many places - Brede, Battle, Hooe, Ninfield, Warbleton, Burwash. At Fairlight, the Overseer of the Poor was bundled into a cart and dumped outside the parish. This symbolic humiliation was reflected in nine other Sussex parishes. At Ringmer Green, Lord Gage met and talked to a vast number of his workers and agreed improved wages. On the same day, Lord Chichester met his labourers at Laughton. In neither case was the meeting other than peaceable.

There were fears, of course, alarming rumours of sinister figures in "drab great coats with velvet collars and top boots", stirring up disorder. The legendary Captain Swing was alleged to ride in a gig, setting fire to ricks and barns with a strange blue spark. But no one ever saw him.

In terms of mob activity, Alfriston remained quiet. There were no serious demonstrations there or in any of the nearby parishes. One young man, William Pearson, was alleged to have assaulted a constable from another parish and to have thereby effected the escape of a Swing rioter who had sought refuge in Alfriston. But even this case was dismissed.

In November 1830 at the height of the Sussex disturbances, a large barn at Berwick Court Farm, tenanted by Richard Saxby, was fired. The glow was seen in the night sky for miles around. Seven loads of wheat, a threshing machine and several large pig pounds were destroyed. Again no culprit was discovered and it is impossible to say if this offence was in any way prompted by the recent rural disturbances. There are strong grounds for suspecting, however, that it was the work of a disgruntled employee, John Reeds, whose record reveals a young man with small regard for the law. The reason for suggesting his guilt is given later.

At the end of October 1831 another fire was reported in the Advertiser.

"On yesterday se'ennight about six o'clock in the evening a fire was discovered in the Parsonage Barn which was entirely consumed with its contents."

The barn, built just behind the church, was rented by two local farmers, John Bodle and William Read. The former's property

".... consisted of 30 quarters of oats, 8 quarters of summer tares, a large quantity of straw and a new waggon, and the property belonging to Mr. Read consisted of 130 bushels of potatoes, some farming tackle and a quantity of straw. The fire was the work of an incendiary and had the wind been in the North East, the Church and the National School must have fallen sacrifice to the flames. From the intense heat many panes of glass in the Church windows were broken."

Again no one was ever charged with this fire.

Incendiarism continued down the years. It is not possible to state its extent because relatively few cases came to court. Although it cannot be verified, there are also suggestions that the press was asked not to report outbreaks. Thus in 1832 one reporter claimed that there was a greater incidence of incendiarism than in 1830. This is not reflected in newspaper reports.

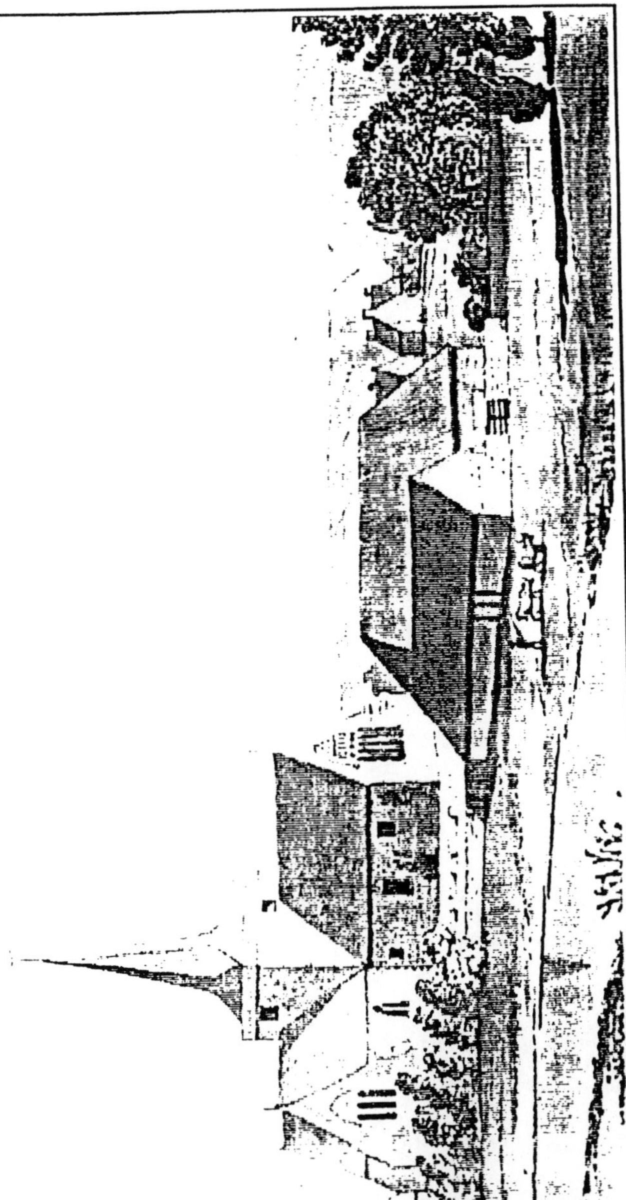

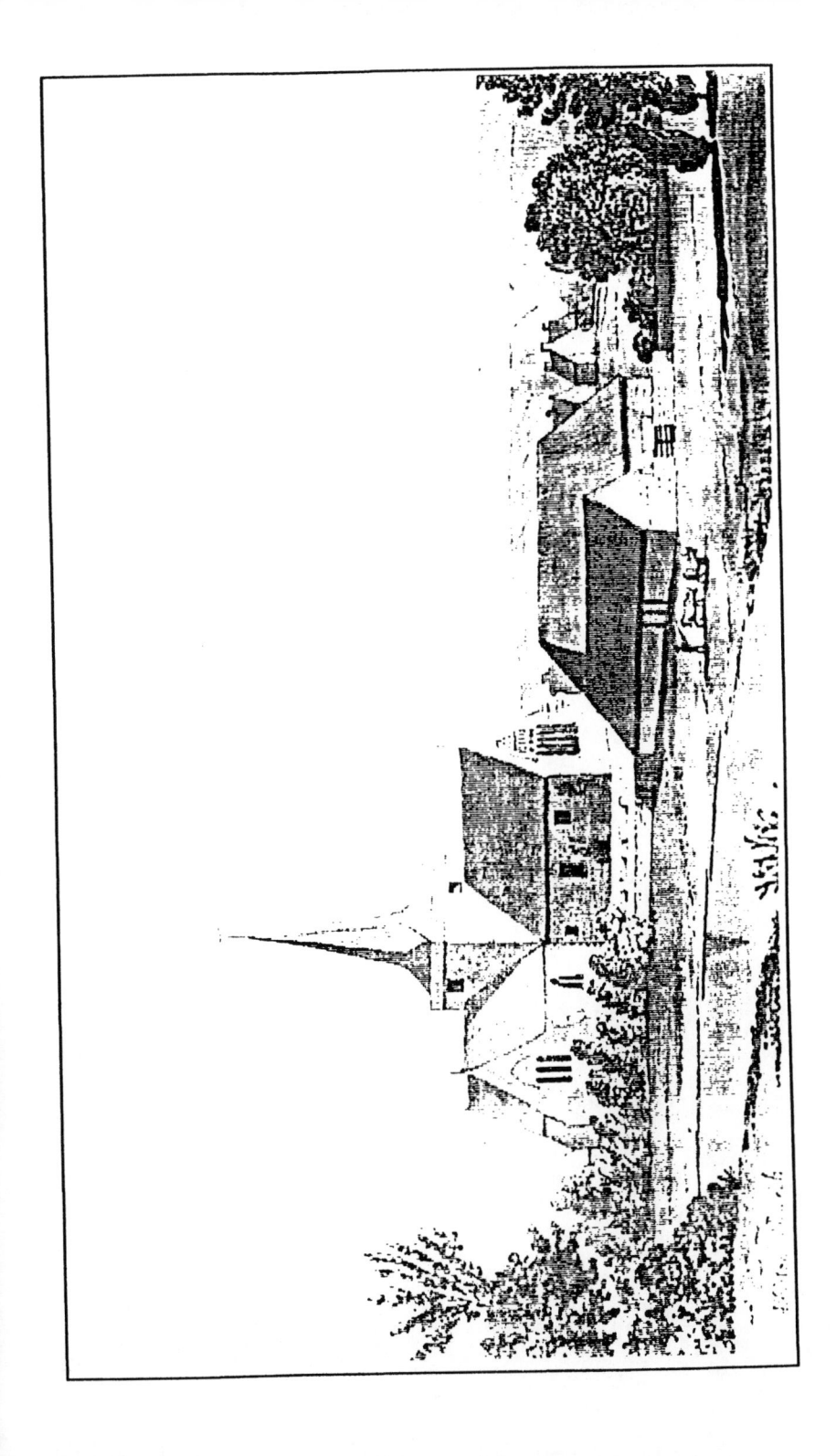

SOME CRIMES : 1830 - 1831

1830

William Pearson, Joseph Wisdom and Edward Cosham were acquitted on a charge of assault on Thomas Reads the elder. The latter had been given such a savage beating "that his life was greatly despaired of".

Pearson, a butcher, was a criminal associate of Collins. In the same year he was acquitted of another assault charge, this time on Thomas Rolf, a constable from Ninfield, who had taken in charge a Swing rioter.

Two years later, Joseph Wisdom, a twenty-four year old carpenter, was acquitted at Brighton on a charge of assault and theft. The two men with him were transported for life.

1831

At the Lewes Spring Assizes the judge revealed how pleased he was that there had been no cases of incendiarism, rioting, machine breaking or even robbery in the eastern part of the county in the first three months of the year. It is as though he was drawing a line under the Swing Riots, as though he thought an evil had been purged. The evidence was, he seemed to be saying, that men had now learnt a lesson and were now seeking to behave themselves.

Joseph Vinall who stole half a gallon of potatoes "of the value of one half penny" from John Woodhams, a miller and maltster of Alfriston, was sentenced to one month's hard labour.

William Pearson was fined £5 for using snares on Deans Place Farm. He "did keep and use eleven wire snares, the same snares being Engines to kill and destroy such Game".

John Reeds, a twenty-two year old, another of Collins' followers, was found guilty of stealing two bushels of oats (7/6) and two bushels of pollard (1/-) from his employer, Richard Saxby, at Berwick Court Farm. He was sentenced to two weeks' solitary confinement and, already regarded as an incorrigible criminal, was ordered to be privately whipped.

Later in the year, Reeds appeared once more in court on a charge of poisoning and killing a foal valued at £2, belonging to his employer. He was found not guilty.

In December of this year, Reeds was a prosecution witness in the case against Lewis Awcock, charged with theft, and in the following year he was principal witness at the trial of his friend Samuel Thorncraft found guilty of the barn fire at Milton Court. As he took part in setting fire to the barn, it seems not unreasonable to ask if he had any knowledge of the burning of his employer's barn at Berwick Court in 1830.

THE TRIALS OF COLLINS AND AWCOCK

On 28th November 1831, the Sussex Advertiser announced that

"... the desperate gang of thieves who have so long with impunity infested Alfriston and its neighbourhood are likely, most of them, to be brought to justice. Some men are in custody on a charge of being connected with a gang, one of whom was arrested on passing through [Lewes] on Saturday night. It is said that some important disclosures have been made, the particulars of which for the ends of justice it may be prudent at present to withhold from the public."

The important disclosures were that Thomas Jenner of Litlington had recognised some sacks stolen from his barn; that the Horsebridge miller, John Gorringe, who had been offered several bushels of barley in the incriminating sacks, had found it prudent to denounce the man who had brought them to his house by night; and that others implicated in this and another theft, realising the game was up, had pointed a finger at the initiator of the crimes.

For years, in Alfriston and its surrounding area, sheep had been taken from fields and corn from barns to be sold elsewhere. The constables and the armed patrols established by the farmers had been unable to prevent these offences. In 1831 matters had been especially bad and despite there being many claiming to know who was behind the thefts, firm evidence of real substance had not been forthcoming. On 21st April 1830 John Newman Brooker, Charles' son, living at that time in London, sent a letter to his sister Anne, wife of George Woodhams, the grocer. He writes: "... I hear that Mr. Stanton [sic] has been having some more of his tricks, he will do it once to [sic] often some day I think".

And now in the early winter of 1831 it was clear that Mr Stanton Collins really had done it once too often. Certainly there had been a considerable number of thefts in recent months, enough crime and disorder to alarm the small local communities. Only days before Collins' arrest, the Advertiser commented:

> "Depredations we are sorry to say continue to prevail at Alfriston. A few nights back two lean sheep were stolen from the small stock of Mr. T. Marchant. On the following night one was also taken from the fold of Mr. John Bodle. About three evenings back a barn belonging to Deans Place Farm was broken open and three sacks of peas carried off, the property of Mrs. Dray. A few nights ago the hives of honey belonging to a poor man named Sawyers, at Milton Street, were carried off and the hives thrown in the river. On Thursday night the cottage of a man named Boniface, a shoemaker, adjoining the public house at Longbridge, was furiously assailed and the whole of the windows with the frames were entirely demolished. The poor man and his wife were sadly alarmed, but nothing availed, the depredators were determined to effect their work of destruction. How these things are allowed to continue is astonishing. There is a Prosecution Society there which musters pretty strong and large Rewards have been offered without effect."

The latter events, the hooliganism, most probably had nothing to do with Collins or with the Alfriston Gang which ought to be regarded as a small body of thieves, stealing to order, on a regular basis and having sure outlets for whatever goods they had stolen. It is , however, possible that young men associated with Collins were responsible for the disorderly behaviour in Milton Street. Men like Samuel Thorncraft and John Reeds who hung around The Royal Oak might well have been involved. Indeed, Thorncraft's sister and her husband and the Reeds and the Bonifaces occupied the three cottages next to the public house.

For the most part the group known as the Alfriston Gang were young men, some seriously criminally inclined, other perhaps in those hard times keen to turn a few shillings. Members who have been identified are: Robert Adams, the three Huggetts (George, James and John), William Trigwell, Lewis Awcock, John Reeds, Samuel Thorncraft, and William Pearson. Some accounts of Collins' gang - and it has to be said that these are not universally reliable - refer to Bob Hall who died in Eastbourne Workhouse aged ninety-four in 1895. But no Hall is ever mentioned in any court cases. In the late 1830s, however, a man of this name, a butcher, was working for William Banks who was then the tenant of Market Cross House. It is possible therefore that Hall worked for Collins as a butcher and in other capacities too.

How many there were in the gang is unknown. But membership of gangs is not a full-time occupation. Even if on very many nights in 1831 the gang was at its work, Pearson and the others were surely not out on every venture. There must have been others whose names have not been recorded.

There is nothing to show how deeply and with what frequency any of the individual members were engaged in thefts organised by Collins. What can be said is that some of the gang had been before the courts on other charges, some on several occasions, and that almost all would face future charges. Three, in addition to Collins, were to be transported. One was to be hanged. There was a desperate and dangerous quality about some of the gang, who appeared in court on charges of assault, although these were not proved in every instance. Certainly when the news spread of Collins' arrest and impending trial there must have been a collective sigh of relief, especially when others associated with him were known to be called in for questioning.

Stanton Collins, aged thirty-five, was committed for trial at Lewes Assizes along with Robert Adams, a twenty-three year old labourer, the son of the former landlord of The George, on a charge of stealing twelve bushels of barley and three sacks, the property of Thomas Jenner of Litlington. The trial of Collins excited great interest "as well from his former respectability as from his supposed leadership of the gang". Equally intriguing was the fact that he was "said to have been possessed of considerable property".

The Brighton Gazette emphasises the degree to which the gang's activities had frightened people in the locality.

"For upwards of twelve months the utmost consternation has prevailed at Alfriston and in its vicinity in consequence of the nocturnal depredations carried off by a gang of thieves who had till now evaded detection."

This was the introduction to the court proceedings as related by the Gazette on 22nd December. The following account of the trial is based largely on that newspaper's reports.

"The farmers, almost nightly, have had their corn, sheep, etc. stolen, yet there was little doubt who they [the thieves] were. Collins, a man of robust and determined appearance, is said to have been at the head of this gang. He has, we believe, been taken up before on suspicion but nothing conclusive was brought against him.

"To such a degree has the alarm prevailed that the inhabitants ... have of late been actually afraid to retire to rest, fearful that before morning they might find their property consumed by fire. The conflagration which took place last week is supposed to have been the work of one of the gang and these suspicions are in some measure confirmed by the witness, Pearson, a late accomplice, who confessed to participation in several robberies but finding, as he observed 'that there was not any living peace' he was induced to turn from his evil ways and to live honestly in future."

The conflagration referred to is that at Milton Court Farm on 11th December. There is, however, no reason to believe that Collins ordered or suggested this or any other outbreaks of arson.

In court, the first witness, Charles Jenner, stated that some sacks of barley had been stolen from his father's barn at Litlington on the night of 11th - 12th November 1831. Two of the sacks were marked with red paint.

The principal witness was Collins' brother-in-law, John Gorringe, whose mill was at Horsebridge, half a dozen miles from Litlington. At about one in the morning he had been wakened by Collins who was accompanied by Robert Adams, calling up to his bedroom window. He had brought three sacks of barley to be ground. Gorringe admitted to being surprised at his brother-in-law's arrival at such an hour. He had refused to come downstairs, telling Collins to put the barley in the shed.

When he had time to inspect them, Gorringe told the court, he noticed that two of the sacks were marked 'T. Jenner' in red paint. The following day Collins and Adams turned up at Gorringe's mill to discuss a price for the barley but they reached no agreement. Collins took away the two marked sacks, leaving the third.

The men met once more at The Plough on Dicker Common, again to resolve the price. Collins asked £4.10s; Gorringe offered £4. In the end they agreed that Collins should take £2 and a quantity of flour.

As yet the barley was not ground and Gorringe and two of his employees, Sam Bearne and Samuel Saunders, all testified that they had had doubts that it had been come by honestly. In court, Saunders' veracity as a witness was challenged: he had recently escaped charges of embezzling a former employer of three small amounts, but he stuck by his story that his master had not ground the barley because he had feared it stolen.

Some years later, Saunders was transported for theft. This though is no proof that he perjured himself in his assuring the court of his and his employer's doubts about the barley's provenance. In any event, whatever he said did not contribute to Collins being found guilty but it might well have saved Gorringe - and Saunders himself - from being found guilty along with Collins.

Somehow, Thomas Jenner, prosecuting the offender, had some information which had led him to Gorringe whom he accused of stealing his barley. It is not clear where this information came from.

The case against Collins was watertight. He offered no defence, aware that he had at last been caught. He was found guilty but no evidence was brought against his accomplice, Robert Adams, who had been one of those anxious to help the authorities now that it seemed all was lost. As for Gorringe, he too jumped clear and Collins seems not to have wanted to implicate his brother-in-law in this or earlier crimes. It is difficult to accept that Collins' midnight visit to Horsebridge was an unusual occurrence or that Gorringe was surprised at his brother-in-law's arrival at such an hour. The truth of the matter seems to be that Collins used

Gorringe as a regular, convenient source for his thefts of grain just as he used Chitty, a Lewes brewer. One might safely assume that he had other outlets, too, for stolen corn and sheep.

Before sentencing Collins, the judge considered a second charge. This time Collins and George Huggett were accused of theft from the Reverend Mr Capper's barn at Burlough Castle, a field in Milton Street with the remains of an ancient enclosure.

As in the case heard immediately before, Collins' former henchmen proved unreliable. Under earlier cross examination, William Pearson had confessed to several robberies. He had undergone a recent change of heart, he told the court.

> "A month ago the depredations having been carried on to a fearful extent," he confessed, "I was induced from repeated solicitations to tell all I know, with a view to putting a stop to these proceedings."

Perhaps this young butcher, who was probably employed by Collins and likely to have lived under his roof, did not express himself quite so grandly. But what he had admitted to before the trial was enough to ensure Collins would be found guilty.

George Huggett, too, though originally charged, was, like Pearson, released without conviction and it has to be assumed that on this occasion he too was supportive of the law.

The theft from Capper's barn was planned in The George by Collins, Huggett and Pearson. The last two had had a preliminary look "to see if there was anything worth having". They had reported back to Collins the result of their reconnaissance. It transpired that there were enough bags of oats to make a visit worthwhile.

Early on the evening of 21st April 1831, Huggett and Pearson took a cart belonging to Collins to Milton Street, leaving it there in readiness for their later visit. At midnight, they collected the cart and took it off the road and up the track. They had no difficulty getting into the barn and taking out the sacks of oats. Collins arrived later and when the cart was finally loaded he and Huggett drove back, Pearson following on foot. At Collins' house in the Square, they unloaded the cart.

At the trial, Ann Herriott who lived opposite Collins, casting her mind back eight months, explained that she thought she had heard a cart outside Collins' house at about two o'clock in the morning.

William Chatfield who lodged with the Herriotts said that on the evening of the theft he had seen Pearson and Huggett with a cart opposite the brick-kiln cottage on the outskirts of Alfriston. The men had seen him looking at the cart and had told him to go away.

"It was a largish, brown cart," Chatfield told the court. "I have seen a similar cart in River Lane." He was sure it was a cart belonging to Collins.

Charles Brooker was also called as a witness at the trial of his enemy. He too had seen the cart on the night in question on his way from Milton Street to Alfriston. But, no, he was unsure that it belonged to Collins. Noble to the end? Perhaps he was aware that his evidence would not matter much. Huggett and Pearson had done all that was necessary.

The jury lost no time in finding Collins guilty.

"The learned judge told the prisoner there was a very good reason to believe that he had placed himself at the head of a gang which had devastated that part of the country in which he resided and it was quite time these fearful depredations should be checked. The prisoner must therefore prepare himself to leave this country."

The sentence of seven years' transportation seems unduly light in comparison with other sentence of transportation for less serious crimes but, neverthless, Collins, "on hearing his sentence looked exceedingly sullen and retired from the bar without uttering a word".

Aware that he would be found guilty, Collins had already prepared for his departure. Prior to the trial he had resold Market Cross House to his father, James, its previous owner. He, in turn, and not without some irony, sold it to Charles Brooker for £800.

Collins is said to have consigned all of his money - several thousand pounds - to his daughter, Katurah. It would otherwise have been forfeit to the Crown as the property of a transportee. Members of the Collins' family still speak of this money, wondering if it may even today be in Chancery. That is a mystery which might be resolved relatively easily.

The only other mystery is what ultimately happened to Collins, his wife Katurah, and his son and daughter, both named after their parents. Several writers have claimed that he returned to this country after serving his time as a convict. They have suggested that he became man-servant to the Reverend Julius Hare, Rector of Herstmonceux. But would Collins, still wealthy, have wished to act in such a capacity? And where was his wife? And the children? None of their names appears in any local registers or census returns.

Elsewhere it is said that he was buried at Wartling in November 1878. But the Stanton Collins there was eighty-nine: our Stanton Collins would have been eighty-four. Nor is he one of the several other Stanton Collins in that part of the county.

Did his wife take the children and the money and join her husband in Australia? Did they all settle there when his sentence expired? There is no proof that this is what happened but it is an interesting possibility.

What can be said with some confidence is that with Collins' departure regular, organised crime, on a scale which seriously frightened and frustrated the community, came to an end. Barns were still raided; sheep were still stolen. But not with the degree of purpose that Stanton Collins had brought to these activities.

Although there are no other accounts of the raids he and his gang carried out, the newspaper reports and the statements of witnesses like Mrs Marchant, Pearson and the judge who sentenced Collins, make it clear that considerable quantities were stolen and that the crimes were conducted with great intensity especially in 1831. Collins' defiance of the community which he might have been expected to serve as an upright member, could end in only one way. Given the sheer volume of offences, it was inevitable that one of the gang members would one day be forced to betray him. It is surprising that no one did so earlier and this only indicates with what impunity offences of the kind could be carried out over a long period of time.

Another member of the Alfriston Gang also faced the judge at the same Assizes as Collins. One of the youths who had been sentenced to three weeks' hard labour for the 'riot' outside Brooker's house three years earlier, had gone on to more ambitious crime. This was Lewis Awcock, found guilty of simple larceny "in the dwelling house of Richard Hasting", the landlord of The George. Hasting was a respectable man who in addition to being the innkeeper was also a plumber/painter/glazier.

A travelling jeweller, Francisco Cometti, had stock valued at £200 stolen while staying at the inn. Awcock was apprehended and charged with stealing the following articles.

1 box	10/-
9 Watches	£50
30 brooches	£30
80 gold rings	£50
60 gold pins	£15
12 gold seals	£9
18 gold watch keys	£7
36 pairs ear drops	£15
32 spoons	£9
1 pr. sugar tongs	15/-
12 oz coral	£3
24 thimbles	30/-
6 pencil cases	£1
4 pr. buckles	4/-
10 pr. bracelets	30/-
12 pr. scissors	12/-
8 knives	8/-
12 watch chains	12/-
18 combs	9/-

This offence is remarkably different from all of the others recorded for Alfriston. What was Awcock intending to do with such a haul? How did he propose to get rid of it? Had he connections in, say, Brighton who could fence it for him? Was it an independent piece of enterprise or one which bore the mark of Collins? It is quite unlike Collins' handiwork. For his part, Awcock is not likely to have had earlier opportunities for a crime of this nature and it does not therefore seem possible that he would know anyone to fence the items. It really does look like an opportunist theft, ambitious enough, but not thought out to its conclusion.

At the trial, evidence for the prosecution not unnaturally was given by Cometti and Hasting. More interestingly, John Reeds gave evidence against Awcock. It is not known if Reeds had participated in the theft and that, in return for a pardon, offered to help the Crown. What else could have caused him to volunteer information? Only weeks later Reeds was once more to give evidence for the prosecution in a major case in which he himself was one of the guilty parties. Whatever the truth of it, Awcock was sentenced to death, a sentence which was commuted to transportation for seven years at the end of the Assizes.

THE EVENTS OF SUNDAY, 11th DECEMBER 1831

Three events occurred in Alfriston on Sunday, 11th December, the eve of Collins' trial. None of the events involved him though his indirect presence hovers in the background of each. One was a 'riot'; the others were fires.

The 'Riot' in the Chapel

On that Sunday, Charles Brooker, senior trustee of the chapel, decided that it was within his power to oust the minister, the Reverend George Betts, who had been at the chapel for the past twenty years. Brooker entered the chapel in the morning and declared Betts dismissed. In his place, Brooker announced, was a 'supply' preacher, Samuel Sands, a turnpike gateman from Milton Street and a regular member of Alfriston Chapel.

Inevitably there was uproar at such high-handed behaviour. Voices were raised; there was shoving, pulling, pushing; fists flew. In the end Brooker's forces were obliged to yield. Sands stepped down from the pulpit, giving way to the Reverend Mr Betts who was reinstated, though only for a few weeks.

Some accounts, notably Geering's, state that a gang of smugglers led by Collins came from The George to support the Betts' faction. Whilst the 'riot', if it lasted long enough, might have offered an opportunity for outsiders to join in, it ought to be recalled that on this particular day Collins was in prison. One of those arrested and later tried and acquitted of a charge of assault in the chapel was Isaac Thorncraft, a regular chapel attender, opposed to Brooker's assumption of power. At the time when Isaac was pulling and pushing and flailing his fists, his brother Samuel was a mile or so away at Levett's beershop in Milton Street. Later that day, Samuel also was to commit an offence that would lead him before the courts.

The 'riot' itself was bizarre. Here was Brooker the schismatic, toppling his own Pope, being his own Henry, trying to resolve his own marriage question.

Brooker's first wife, Elizabeth Newman, had died of tuberculosis. His second wife, Ann Ellis, was only twenty-three when she died in 1827. Now Brooker wished to take as his third wife, Mary Ellis, sister of Ann. It was over this that he had clashed with Betts who opposed a marriage to so close a relative. Samuel Sands was more pliant. He saw nothing scripturally wrong in such a union. This persuaded Brooker that he should take action.

The 'riot' in the chapel afforded local Anglicans much amusement. One wonders, however, why Brooker's normally sound judgement was so flawed on this occasion. He was generally shrewd, a man of sharp insight, politically astute. Had the events of past weeks in some way distorted his ideas? Had the arrest of Stanton Collins, the fact that Collins in the next week would undoubtedly be found guilty, so elated Brooker, so filled him with confidence that he was emboldened to embark on so rash an act? Perhaps in this sense Collins had influenced events.

One result of the intemperate manner in which Brooker had acted was that the chapel was split, a whole group seceding to Sevencrofts barn with Betts. Over the next few months there were further resignations from Brooker's chapel whilst others returned from Sevencrofts. The Minute Book records that some left "owing to an unpleasant feeling towards Mr. C. Brooker occasioned by the late affair at the Chapel relative to the Rev. G. Betts". In October 1832, the "late affair" still rumbling, there was "a special Church Meeting held for prayer and humiliation before God to pardon the iniquity of the late disgraceful and riotous proceedings at the Church".

Memories of the chapel 'riot' lasted long and the Sevencrofts group continued their meetings in their barn in Star Lane for several years.

Attempted Arson at Brooker's Warehouse

Some time in the evening of that same Sunday an attempt to set fire to Brooker's warehouse failed. Were the culprits disgruntled chapel members? Unlikely. Were they friends of

Collins? Were they labourers opposed to Brooker in his capacity as an influential member of the Vestry and one of those whom they held responsible for low rates of relief? There is no telling: the culprits were never found.

The Fire at Milton Court Farm

Early on the same evening, across the river at Milton Street, Charles Ade's barn was set alight. A letter of 17th December, from the agent of the Earl of Plymouth to Lord Melbourne, Home Secretary, describes the progress of the enquiry, stating:

> ".... that there at present exists and has for a considerable time a Gang of very bad Character in that Neighbourhood who are setting at defiance the ordinary means at the disposal of such Owners to detect and bring them to justice."

But by now Collins had been tried and sentenced and perhaps it was already believed that the gang had suffered a serious setback, as indeed it had.

> "On the evening of Sunday the 11th Instant," the letter continues, "some very Valuable Farm Buildings and Ricks upon a Farm in the parish of Milton were burnt down and from a very active Investigation since made and still in progress, the Magistrates, Messrs. Courthorpe and Geer of Lewes, feel convinced that this Fire was the Act of Incendiaries, part of the Gang above mentioned."

Already a reward of £200 was on offer but the writer had a further proposal to make on behalf of the Earl and other influential landowners.

> "It is felt however that this Object would be materially assisted by their being authorised to promise His Majesty's Pardon to any of the Parties giving Information of

his Confederates with a further Reward upon Conviction."

Within days, the Sussex Advertiser was able to report:

"THE MILTON FIRE - The three men in custody, charged with being concerned in this diabolical transaction, are named John Reads [sic], Samuel Thorncraft and Samuel Miller, all agricultural labourers. They have undergone several private examinations .... A man named Samuel Lower is also in custody and has been examined on suspicion of being concerned in placing a ball of combustible matter nigh to a stack on another farm in the neighbourhood of Alfriston on the same evening as the destructive fire at Milton occurred."

Samuel Lower was never charged with attempted arson at a local farm. Was this a case of misreporting? Was it Brooker's warehouse which Lower was accused of trying to fire? Or were there on that evening three distinct sets of incendiaries abroad?

MILTON FIRE.

Near Alfriston.

£200.
REWARD.

WHEREAS
On SUNDAY EVENING last,
THE

BARNS
AND RICKS,

At Milton Farm, in the Parish of Arlington, Were maliciously SET on FIRE.

Whoever will give Information against the Offender or Offenders, so that he or they may be brought to Justice, shall receive TWO HUNDRED POUNDS REWARD, over and above all other Rewards; to be paid on Conviction.

F. H. GELL.

LEWES, 12th December, 1831.

BAXTER, PRINTER, LEWES.

THE TRIAL OF SAMUEL THORNCRAFT, 1832

The enquiries into the Milton Court Farm fire were successfully concluded probably before Christmas although the case was not tried until March 1832.

The newspapers carry full accounts of the trial although at the same sessions there was greater interest in charges against Ann Kennett, accused of harbouring the Brighton wife-murderer, John Holloway. He had been found guilty at the previous Assizes and had since been executed. Nevertheless, the trial of an Alfriston man, so hard on the heels of the proceedings against Collins only four months earlier, excited enough attention.

"The prisoner is an exceedingly fine made man," the Brighton Gazette informed its readers, "and his jet black hair and whiskers, with a scowling eye, and a determined and resolute appearance rendered him an object of much attention.

When asked how he pleaded, Thorncraft replied, "that he wished to be tried by the laws of his country to see if he could be proved guilty. The question was again put to him but he remained silent."

The prosecution was initiated by the Earl of Plymouth, that forever absent landlord, on behalf of his tenant, Charles Ade. The fire had consumed a three-floored barn - described by Ade as three barns in one - some other buildings and an ox stall. Also lost were 36 quarters of wheat, 150 quarters of barley, 20 quarters of peas and three hay stacks. Only a little wheat and barley was saved.

On the evening of the fire, Ade had been sitting in his parlour when he heard a horse gallop past the window. Looking out, he saw the barn on fire. So fierce was the blaze that within fifteen minutes the three floors of the building had collapsed and the roof had fallen in.

Very quickly, within days, Samuel Thorncraft was arrested and charged. He was, in fact, in custody along with his accomplice,

John Reeds, before the Earl of Plymouth's agent wrote to Melbourne on the 17th December. Four days after the fire on the Thursday, Thorncraft's brother-in-law's house was searched by Joseph Ticehurst, said to be a detective. Acting upon information given him by Reeds on 15th December, he had found a tinder box with steel, flint and a small piece of deal in a kitchen cupboard. On a shelf there was a scallop shell in which brimstone had been melted. This was not conclusive proof of guilt: such items were to be found as essential in all homes. What is important here is that Thorncraft was so quickly a suspect and the details of the case against him were so soon being drawn up.

Thorncraft, a twenty-two year old, had been employed by Ade for several years. He was not the best of workers, a man who at times took time off to go drinking. At the trial a witness referred to the accused man being in Banks' beer shop in North Street in Alfriston when he ought to have been at work just days before the fire. As his master rode by, Thorncraft had ducked down out of sight. Yet in spite of his imperfections as an employee, he continued in Ade's employ over at least five years. Reeds, too, at the time of his arrest seems to have been employed by Ade in spite of his bad record which was obviously common knowledge.

Some years earlier, Ade - "a most respectable farmer," says the Brighton Gazette, "who has ever proved himself the poor man's friend" - had prosecuted Thorncraft for the theft of seven apples. The seventeen year old went to prison for a month. Whilst it had nothing directly to do with his work, Thorncraft had served another month in prison as the prime mover in the 'riot' in front of Brooker's house. More recently, in November, only weeks before the fire at Milton Court, Ade had taken Thorncraft before a magistrate in Lewes, accusing him of stealing six sacks of wheat. He could provide no evidence, however, to support his accusation and the charge was not proceeded with. In the succeeding weeks, the young labourer was to complain about how unjustly treated he had been in this matter.

After examination at Lewes in December 1831, Thorncraft confessed to having fired the barn at Milton Court but claimed that the idea had been put to him by John Reeds who was "always drawing it into his head". At the time he had been drunk, he said, otherwise he would never have burnt his master's property. Mr Ade had always been good to him, he assured his interrogators.

If Thorncraft wished to implicate Reeds he was too late. His accomplice had already offered his account - which is probably accurate - to the authorities. Just as in the case of Lewis Awcock at the previous Assizes, Reeds was on hand with his evidence. Either two were to hang or one. That much was plain. Reeds, by volunteering his account of what had occurred, ensured that it would be only one.

The case against Thorncraft was overwhelmingly strong. Several witnesses claimed to have heard him make incriminating remarks. Charles Smith told the court that in the early hours of 12th December, when efforts were still being made to fight the fire, he had talked to Thorncraft at The Royal Oak. If Ade asked why he was not helping to fight the fire, Smith said, "he would d----d soon tell him".

Sarah Young who lived with her son, the landlord of The Royal Oak - not yet William Ford - had heard Thorncraft speak against his employer several times when he was drunk. "Some time before the fire", but she could not say how long, she heard the prisoner say he did not care "if Mr. Ade turned him away - if his master turned him away he would set every bloody building he had alight".

On another occasion, he had told fifteen year old William Weller, who worked with him, that he had not stolen his master's wheat, that he had been falsely accused and that "he would pay Mr. Ade off for it".

There had been talk that Ade intended to dismiss Thorncraft. With some show of bravado, Thorncraft had boasted to the tailor, James Young: "Mr. Ade knows better than to discharge me".

Young and others had also heard him sing the doggerel lines:

> "Collins is merry there
> And we be merry here
> And set the barns
> About their ears."

Then there was the steel Joseph Ford had dropped some weeks earlier in a friendly wrestling bout and which Thorncraft had picked up. Young had seen him show it to Mercy Cox, telling her, "I don't care as long as you don't get that for that is what I set the barns and hovels on fire with". Was Thorncraft serious? Was he confessing his responsibility for other outbreaks?

And was he expressing an opinion based on personal experience when one day, talking about the buildings at Milton Court, he said to Michael Winchester, another workmate, "If anybody set fire to that corner of the barn it would soon devour the lot"?

Reeds told the court what had led up to the fire and he described the eventual commission of the crime. On the Saturday night, the two men had been at Levett's beershop in Milton Street from eight o'clock until eleven. They were drunk when they returned to Thorncraft's house where they slept.

By ten o'clock the next morning they were drinking once more at Levett's. Some time in the afternoon they went across to The Royal Oak. On their way over to the public house Thorncraft told Reeds, apparently not for the first time, that if his master dismissed him, he would fire his barn.

It was then at The Royal Oak that James Young saw Thorncraft show the steel to Mercy Cox and later heard him singing about firing barns.

After drinking more beer, Thorncraft went outside. Reeds' evidence continued:

> "About four I went out and found the prisoner in the high road. He said, 'Have you a mind to go?'
> "I said, 'I don't care.'
> "He asked if I had got the tinder and flint. I said yes. I got father's unknown to him. Prisoner said he had got a flint. He went to his sister's and got a bunch of matches: we went over to Brig Meadow and across to Milton barn, and when there, went into the ox-stall which was fastened with a catch; prisoner opened the door; I struck a light; he lit the matches and told me to be off and I went away; he came after me and said it would not catch; he said he would go down to his sister's and get some more tinder, matches and a piece of candle; when there he said he wanted some tinder; she said she had not got any but

she could make some. Samuel Miller then went upstairs and fetched a box; prisoner then took the tinder out and put it on a piece of paper; he asked for matches; she said she had not got any more; she said she would make some; she then got a piece of wood; she and the prisoner cut some like other matches; she dipped the matches into the scallop shell in which there was melted brimstone; the prisoner asked for a piece of candle but I did not see it given him."

But the Millers? Did they not pause to ask why they were being asked for these items? Was this usual? Did they not even for a moment ask why two half-drunk young men had called on them with such requests? Presumably the Millers had heard Samuel's boasts and threats. Did they not for one moment suspect what was in his mind?

Thorncraft and Reeds separated at this point and did not meet again until about seven o'clock. In the intervening two or three hours, they had not rethought their plan, had not dismissed it as a foolhardy product of their drinking. At seven o'clock, they were as resolute as they had been several hours earlier.

Reeds tells how he met Thorncraft again.

"It was near The Royal Oak; the prisoner and I went over the green meadow; we went towards Alfriston as far as the ash tree; we then went across to the barn; prisoner told me he had got tinder, matches and candle; we both went in at the stall; I struck the light; he lit the matches and told me to be off.

"I went away. I saw him put the matches in the peas mow; I went over to the rick settle; prisoner came after me and told me it had caught; we then ran across the green meadow; he told me he had the steel of J. Ford; he said he had got plenty of witnesses to show that it was Ford's steel; we went across the green field; I could not keep up with him so he stopt for me on the causeway. He said then, 'Now we must go back,' but we did not but ran across a ploughed field and lay in a hedge."

The hand-drawn map which was used at the trial carries the faintest pencil note. Above the line of hedge which ran along the path from Winton Street and down Sloe Lane into Alfriston, someone has written:

"Bushes where the prisoners are said to have run to after having set fire to the barn &c."

Reeds' deposition continues:

"We stopt a minute; he said we must not stop here or they will say it is us; so we ran back to the fire as far as we could and he got there first. I stopped there all night."

Reed implies that he busied himself, helping to douse the flames. Thorncraft seems not to have given any assistance at the blaze and hours later, at two in the morning, still at The Royal Oak, he was assuring Charles Smith of the response he would give his employer if he was asked why he was not fighting the fire. And some time during the evening or the early hours of morning he had sought out Joseph Ford. "That's yours, I believe," he had said, taking the steel out of his pocket and offering it to its owner.

Thorncraft had had it in mind on the night of the fire to implicate Joseph Ford. Reeds referred to that in his evidence. Ade's claim that Thorncraft had stolen some sacks of wheat had apparently resulted from information given by Ford. Exactly how Thorncraft's possession of Ford's steel and his later returning it would prove the latter's guilt is unclear.

Thorncraft was found guilty as charged. His father, John, standing up in court with tears in his eyes, implored the judge to forgive his son. "He would send him thousands and thousands of miles away, never to do so any more, as he had an opportunity of getting the poor fellow taken to America".

A useless plea.

"The judge then putting on the fatal black cap, in a very impressive and solemn manner pronounced the

Alfriston

School

Bank's Beer-shop
Gibson

Chapel

Long Bridge

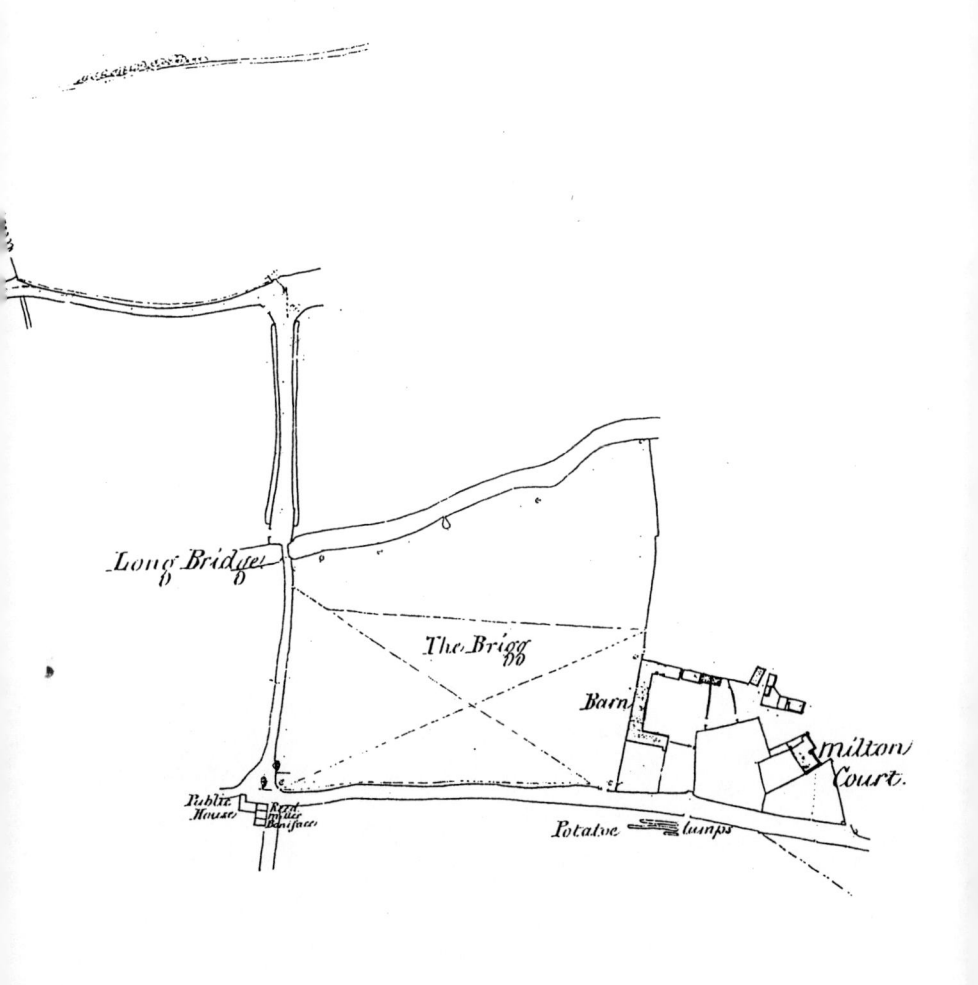

The Brigg

Barn

Milton Court

Public House

St. Boniface

Potatoe lumps

sentence of death, observing that the prisoner had been found guilty of a most heinous offence which crime, if suffered to escape the severity of the law, would render the habitation of man no longer a place of safety; that his case had been aggravated by a long-concealed malignity. His lordship then informed the prisoner that he could hope for no mercy on this side of the grave, and exhorted him to devote the short remaining period of his existence to the duties of religion."

Thorncraft's demeanour throughout the trial is said to have been calm and dignified. Only once did he call out to accuse one of the witnesses of lying. His only other recorded comment is that which he made to John Reeds at the end of the trial. Several in the court, including some of the women who had testified against him, had pressed forward and shaken his hand. Only when John Reeds offered his hand did Thorncraft refuse with the words that "he would rather be tucked up here than tell as many lies as he had told".

Whatever we may think of Reeds - and his record is not good - his account of what occurred on 11th December must be broadly true. He does not deny, could not deny, his part in what happened at Milton Court barn. But to find Reeds on the side of those who would hang him was undoubtedly difficult for Thorncraft to stomach.

In the meantime, there was some feeling of relief in the locality after the arrests of so many law-breakers, even if only three suffered punishment. Mrs Ann Marchant, in a letter to her sister Mrs Sophie Peskett on 8th January 1832, wrote of her qualified relief at the change in events.

"... We have been quite in commotion for some time past breaking up a Gang of Thieves and as you see by the papers have secured some but am sorry to say there are still many left, tho' I'm much in hopes now their depredations will be put a stop to, as we have a Patrol lately established and every exertion making [sic] to discover and bring to Justice the Guilty. We were dreadfully alarmed with the fires and have no doubt but the greater part of Alfriston would have been consumed before the winter had ended had they not been arrested in their progress as they seemed bent on destruction."

Like many others, Mrs Marchant saw arson as part of a plot, motivated in equal parts by malice, evil, greed and resentment. Perhaps she saw the whole social order about to collapse. Had not France and other parts of Europe experienced dreadful revolution in the last two years or so? No doubt she hoped that matters would settle down now even though not all of the villains had been brought to book. In the next few months she would feel some relief at the departure of Collins and she might hope that the awful example of Thorncraft and even that of Lewis Awcock would deter those still abroad, the likes of Pearson, Reeds, William Trigwell, the Huggetts, and others whose names and characters are unknown to us but who would be well known to her.

Many years later Ellman wrote:

"In the riots of 1830 [sic] a half-witted lad was tried and hung for burning a barn at Milton Court. When I took charge of Lullington in 1839, I found there residing the man who had turned King's evidence against him, and who I understood had first decoyed the poor imbecile to join him in the crime, and then to save his own neck, had given him up to the gallows."

Was Thorncraft half-witted, an imbecile? No other source suggests this and the newspaper reports describe him as a dignified figure in the court room. What is interesting is that Reeds could continue living in Lullington, presumably in the same house, so many years after having appeared in court twice in the space of a few weeks to condemn local men.

Thorncraft was hanged at Horsham on 3rd April 1832. Typically the newspaper reports concentrate on the consolations he found in his religion so that "he never indulged in the slightest hope of escape from the awful end that awaited him but evinced the greatest firmness and fortitude and paid the utmost attention to the religious instruction which was constantly administered to him by the Revd. Mr. Witherby, the worthy chaplain of the gaol".

On the morning of his execution, Thorncraft's parents and his brother-in-law, Samuel Miller, visited him. The Sussex Advertiser devotes much space to the harrowing occasion. Thorncraft, composed throughout we are told, assured his visitors that he was prepared for death and did not fear it. He expressed regrets for his past behaviour, blaming drink for his present plight. His parents were to ensure that his brothers did not follow the path he had taken.

"The appointed time having nearly arrived for the execution, they embraced each other for the last time and the separation of the mother was truly distressing but Thorncraft retained the greatest fortitude.

"At twelve o'clock the Governor conducted the criminal from the condemned cell across the yard to the press-room where the executioner performed the ceremony of pinioning, during which time the miserable man did not utter a sentence. The awful preparations being completed, the large folding doors in front of the prison were thrown open and, preceded by the Revd. Mr. Witherby, who commenced reading the burial service, the mournful procession moved towards the drop, the culprit walking with a firm step and evidently wishing the ceremony as brief as possible. Having arrived at the foot of the drop, he ascended the platform without evincing the slightest emotion. The executioner now placed him under the fatal beam and the composure and fortitude which he still preserved astonished the spectators. His attitude might be called graceful, his position was like that of a soldier standing at ease ... The executioner asked Thorncraft if he wished to address the people. He replied 'No'. The question being repeated, he again, but in more emphatic tone, said 'No'. Shortly afterwards the signal was given, the drop fell, and the ill-fated man was launched into eternity. His struggles were of longer duration than is usually the case, which was probably owing to the bungling manner in which the executioner had prepared his duty, who upon this occasion did not, as is the custom take hold of the criminal's legs to shorten the period of his sufferings. After the body had hung the usual time, it was taken down and placed in a coffin which had been prepared by the relatives who accompanied it in a cart to Alfriston for interment.

"Thorncraft was a remarkably fine young man, only twenty two years of age.

"There were but few spectators to witness the execution. They did not amount in number to 300."

SOME CRIMES : 1832 - 1833

1832

Only weeks after the Collins' verdict and while Samuel Thorncraft was still awaiting trial, the following report appeared in the Sussex Advertiser of 16th January:

"Though there has been a nightly patrol established at Alfriston, and which is in a full operation, there seems an inveteracy for thieving there, and this we think will evidently appear ...... when we state that the warehouse of Mr. C. Brooker was attempted to be broken into about half past one o'clock on the morning of Sunday se'nnight. The thieves first made a small hole through the warehouse door, apparently to ascertain where the bar of the door was; having ascertained this they made a large hole (about large enough for the introduction of a man's hand) through the door towards its edge, where the bar fastens and, probably, through the introduction of the hand, had very nearly succeeded in gaining admission by these means when the barking of the shop dog aroused Mr. B's shopman who immediately hastened to the warehouse, and the thieves, finding they were discovered, made off down the lane towards the Tye or the Tanyard. The same premises of Mr.B. were attempted, but providentially prevented, to be set on fire on the same evening the fire took place at Milton, by a fireball made of candle cotton and which no doubt had been prepared for the purpose, by being impregnated with some strong spirituous liquid. A question to be raised is whether the attempt on the warehouse was for the purpose of thieving or incendiarism. It is supposed that the depredators, in order to effect their purpose, watched the patrol when they for a short period were taking some refreshment."

The following item appeared in the Sussex Advertiser of 13th February:

> "At the latter end of last week, three or four sheep skins with wool, were found in Mr. Brooker's Tan Hill at Alfriston, no doubt deposited there by the Alfriston Gang, many sheep having been stolen in the neighbourhood in the last eight or ten months. The skins were in a state of decomposition."

The fact that Collins had gone did not stop the press from referring to the Alfriston Gang.

John and James Huggett, both criminal associates of Collins, were charged with the theft of fourteen bushels of wheat and one sack belonging to a farmer in Framfield. Because material witnesses could not be traced the case was postponed to the next Assizes. There is no record of any subsequent trial.

In March the Sussex Advertiser reported:

> "A few nights since seven fowls were stolen from a hovel on Deans Farm, Alfriston, in the occupation of Mr. Dray. The thieves were detected in the act of stealing the fowls by the Alfriston nightly patrol, some of whom entered the hovel at the same time. The robbers, however, escaped!"

1833

An Alfriston labourer, John Glover, was sentenced to six months' hard labour for stealing money from William Hughes.

POOR LAW, WORKHOUSE AND FIRE : 1834 - 1835

The Poor Law Act of 1834 was designed by a Government struggling to come to terms with turbulent social change. The old order could not cope with the population increase, the economic depression and the worrying growth of what today would be called a dependency culture among the poor. In Sussex in the 1820s and 1830s, 14% of the rural population were classed as paupers, relying on relief.

John Ellman of Glynde, one of that great Sussex farming family, who had a reputation for caring for his workers, was quite capable of holding a totally blinkered view of the agricultural workers' plight when they were either unemployed or underemployed. When the Poor Law amendments were under discussion, he wrote:

> "Let us hope that some plan may be adopted to make the lower classes feel that they must depend on their own exertions; that they are not entitled to relief, when ill or old, if they have it in their power to lay by for the evil hour ... those who have saved nothing are just as well off when they get the parish claim."

But when did the vast majority of agricultural workers ever have it in their power to lay by enough for the evil hour? Now, the accepted customs of centuries, the obligations of masters to men, rich to poor, were no longer in place. The poor had been rejected by the upper echelons of a rural hierarchy. There was now a disdain for the poor, for their way of life, for their seeming lack of foresight. They were charged with being responsible through their fecklessness for their own ills.

In September 1834 Assistant Commissioner Hawley arrived in the county to implement the new legislation, the aim of which was to provide relief at the lowest cost to the ratepayers. His advice to magistrates was clear: "By a strict adherence to this system," he told them, "you will find that you will shortly get rid of some of your worst and most idle characters." The system was to cut down on outdoor relief within the parish. Now the poor, if they could no longer feed, clothe, heat and house themselves, would be sent to the workhouse.

If they did not end up in the workhouse, it would be because they were at least providing for themselves. Hawley expected the magistrates to act with ruthlessness towards those applying for relief. It was this harshness which promoted a new wave of rural crime. In 1834 and 1835 arson, animal stealing and maiming, as well as theft of farm property was on the increase. And Hawley was wrong too: many would prefer to starve at home rather than face the harsh, inhuman spirit of the workhouse.

Charles Brooker, who as a leading member of the Vestry, had suffered personal abuse, damage to his property and theft from his shop in the 1820s and early 1830s now emerged as a supporter of working men and their families and an opponent of the new Act and its workhouses. This was no sudden turnabout. Brooker, stiff necked and obdurate though he might be, had strong Christian sympathies for the poor and the injustices they were experiencing. 'Retrospect of an Age', a poem he wrote in the late 1830s, focused on the conditions of the poor. Two lines read:

"... Yet I feel her poor slaves
                still do groan.
When, when shall their
                manacles fall?"

Opposing the Act and all it implied, Brooker's aim was to destroy it, to ensure that the manacles fell. This brought him into confrontation with local farmers led by Henry Pagden of Frog Firle. They were grateful that a real attempt to reduce the rates was at last being made. They approved wholeheartedly of the centralisation of the administration and organisation of poor relief. Bigger units of local government, they believed, were more efficient, more cost-effective. They were more alarming too, more frightening. In the eyes of some of the Act's supporters, this was one of its virtues.

Brooker launched his campaign against the new Poor Law with meetings in Alfriston and other villages. He addressed meetings whenever and wherever he could, claiming to have the support of "the Working People". "The Trade or rather the Householders are for me," he declared. It was "a combination of agriculturalists" who were acting against the interests of working people.

After being elected to the newly formed Board of Poor Law Guardians, which he hoped to destroy from within, his election was declared invalid. It was said that he did not have appropriate property qualifications. Odd that a man owning a dozen or so houses in Alfriston should be found wanting, but a loophole to exclude him had been found by Pagden and Dray. Brooker's place on the Board was taken by Pagden whom he had defeated in the election.

Turned away from the inaugural meeting of the Board at Eastbourne in April 1835, Brooker faced a hero's welcome when he returned to Alfriston where he was met by a band and "a considerable concourse .... with banners and mottoes".

Later Brooker took a petition to Somerset House, hoping to present it to Edward Chadwick, Secretary of the Poor Law Commission, but he was refused access. It was important, however, that he continue his struggle. During this period of activity, it was reported that the red flag and another inscribed 'Death or Liberty' flew in Alfriston.

What is incalculable is the degree to which activities like those of Brooker were instrumental in channelling the anger and resentment of working people into a political movement and away from the raw reactions of damage and theft. There was, for example, an embryo trade union, The United Brothers of Industry, which drew up its aims and code of behaviour and many agricultural workers saw hope in this. Most after all were not involved in lawlessness and deplored many of the acts of dishonesty and violence being enacted in villages throughout the land.

Shortly before his death in 1843 Brooker, who had single-mindedly pursued his aims, wrote:

> "We have heard of the Alfriston Gang and no wonder that persons have been sent abroad for outrageous proceedings in Alfriston; pity, it seems, that a few more, as associates to accompany them, had not been shipped off from Alfriston."

He meant, of course, Pagden, Dray, King, Woodhams and the others whom he had opposed in their support of the workhouse system and who in turn had organised a boycott of his already ailing tannery and the grocer's shop of George Woodhams, his son-in-law.

It is not surprising that crimes of need and crimes of revenge marked the period and that landowners and farmers, who had forfeited the loyalty of past generations of their workmen, were often targeted. When The Times correspondent wrote of Sussex in 1835 that "a rankling feeling of discontent and a diabolical spirit of revenge prevailed over a large proportion of the peasantry" he did not evidence any sympathy for thousands of families in dire need. Their responses he believed to be unreasonable and ungrateful. Nor did farmers show much sympathy for their workers although at times they were somewhat selective in those they prosecuted. Even those they took to court continued in their employment. Reeds, Thorncraft in his time, the Russells and others guilty of lesser offences were charged, fined or imprisoned for stealing their masters' property and then returned to work at the same farms. This is difficult to explain in a time of labour surplus. Perhaps some prosecutions were simply token demonstrations of the employers' potential strength. Or was it the reverse? In the end, were employers afraid to take the ultimate sanction, afraid to dismiss those of their workers who were too dangerous to be too severely punished with dismissal?

Woodhams, King, Ade, Dray, all prosecuted men for relatively minor offences at times. In turn they were visited frequently by sheep rustlers and animal maimers. Pagden suffered a fire so serious that the Brighton Gazette expressed the view that the offence "almost warrants the belief that the character of the English peasantry is entirely changed in the present day".

Perhaps the peasants were changed; perhaps they felt bitter in a way they had never felt before; perhaps they believed themselves betrayed in a way they had never known before. Their conditions had never been worse and what they had come to regard for generations as their entitlement to relief had been snatched from them. Nevertheless, violence was rare and it was mainly ricks and barns and not houses and people which suffered.

Naturally there were those in Alfriston who would concur with the Brighton Gazette's and The Times' disapproval of the labourers. The Reverend Charles Day in a letter to Wellington in 1834 declared that the village was "famous for its disaffection ... for years a scourge to the Neighbourhood". The vicar, the Reverend Charles Bohun Smith, told Mrs Ellman on one occasion: "The devil is in this place". Hawley commented that the village was notorious "for the bad Character of its inhabitants". In another letter to her sister in 1834, Mrs Marchant wrote: "I should be delighted to move from this more than ever hateful place".

On Sunday, 2nd November 1834, Tile Barn at Frog Firle, Pagden's farm, was fired. Barley, the whole produce of the harvest, three out of four large wheat stacks, sheds and some recently built bullock lodges were lost in addition to the barn. A fire engine from Bishopstone Tide Mill and a smaller one from Burnt House, belonging to John King, arrived too late. Loss and damage were initially assessed at £700.

The Brighton Gazette found the attack on such "a highly respectable tenant" incomprehensible, "from the fact that he is considered by the labouring classes a kind master". When was a tenant farmer not so considered? Ade had been similarly lauded at the time of the Milton Court fire.

Some days after the fire, Pagden received a letter purporting to come from a friend and warning him not to go out at night. The letter hinted that others were likely to suffer as he had done.

Hardly surprisingly, John Reeds was arrested, but after being questioned, he was released. Then a reward of £158 was offered. The Reverend Mr Day wrote to Wellington asking him to increase the sum although he admitted that it would not be claimed "because the Incendiary is believed departed for America". Day's reasoning was that an increased reward might "prevent the recurrence of Incendiary Acts and stimulate the Neighbourhood to increased exertions". He referred to the problem of insurance which was placing pressure on the finances of many farmers. "I have been endeavouring to get insurance effected to the further account of £2000 for Mr. Pagden but the Office decline negotiating".

The search for the Frog Firle arsonists came to nothing. The name of whoever it was who had fled to America is not known today though perhaps at the time it was common enough knowledge. Other fires, notably at Chyngton where the largest barn in the county was burnt out, flared throughout the area. A reward of £150 was on offer at Chyngton but no one was ever charged. Many other fires were too insignificant even to merit a mention in the press.

Animals, usually sheep, were also targets, either stolen or maimed. Maiming was in general an act of protest. Dray at Deans Place had a number of his animals maimed in 1835. Some animals were killed and skinned on the spot; the best cuts were taken and the skin, head and entrails left as a reminder of the labourers' small power. Other sheep went direct to butchers at 10/- a carcass.

Two London policemen, Ryan and Hall, arrived on the local scene but produced little in the way of evidence for whoever had hired them - The Norwich or Sun Fire; landowners' associations; magistrates. The detectives' presence failed to prevent continued criminal activities against farmers. Disguised as sailors or farm labourers, Ryan and Hall listened, looked, asked questions of those they identified as potential informants. But who would talk to strangers about such matters?

And so the "depredations and wanton outrage" went on. According to some they were the result of "the machinations of desperate Characters in Alfriston". Not the old gang of desperate characters, of course. Now it was Brooker, accused of inciting workers to commit criminal acts against their employers. It seemed that strait-laced, puritanical, stubborn Brooker had inherited the mantle of Stanton Collins.

But Brooker's anger kept him going. Images like those reported in the radical Brighton Patriot kept his anger hot.

> "Our workhouse is just filling with poor families from the different parishes of our Union. It is heart-rending to see the hollow cheeks of the males and the careworn countenances of the females who have been dragging out an existence for several weeks (without employment or relief) on a scanty allowance of potatoes and cold water to slake their thirst, hoping every day they would produce something to keep them from the Whig prison."

In that autumn and winter of 1834, some of Alfriston's poor were given work digging the fields at £2 an acre. The children helped by putting wheat seeds in the holes in the ground made by their brothers and fathers. But there was not work for all and the workhouse and ever more grinding poverty beckoned.

Not only was Brooker's anger hot. So was that of many labouring families. Some responded in the only way they believed open to them.

£158 REWARD.

WHEREAS,

Some evil-disposed Person or Persons, did, in the night of SUNDAY, the 2nd November instant, wilfully & maliciously

SET FIRE
TO A
BARN, LODGE,
AND
WHEAT STACKS,

of Mr **HENRY PAGDEN**, at **Frogfirle**, in Alfriston, whereby the same were consumed.

Any Person who will give Information of the Offender or Offenders, so that he or they may be brought to Justice, shall receive a Reward of £100 from the UNION PROSECUTING SOCIETY, over and above the Reward of £58 from the under-mentioned SUBSCRIBERS; such Rewards respectively to be paid upon Conviction.

By Order of the Society,

F. H. GELL, Treasurer.

LEWES, 8th November, 1834.

Members of the Union Prosecuting Society.

SUBSCRIBERS.

Baxter, Printer, Lewes.

SOME CRIMES : 1834 - 1837

1834

Charles Miller, George Russell, James Russell and John Russell were found guilty of the theft of a cask of beer (10/-) from Thomas Berry and 18 gallons of beer (18/-) and two bushels of sharps (flour not of the highest grade) from William Banks, the mealman and beershop owner.
All received two months' hard labour.

Richard Saunders, a twenty-one year old labourer, was acquitted of stealing a lamb (10/-) from Berwick Court Farm. (In 1838, along with Henry Hudson, a gardener, he was transported for seven years for the theft of a dozen fowl valued at 32/-.)

William Pettit was accused of the theft of five tame fowls at Deans Place Farm on Christmas Eve 1834. Mrs Hilder had seen the birds during the day "in front of my Brother William Dray's Barn Doors near to the lodge in which they roost".
Samuel Herriott's deposition, signed not unusually with a cross, states that he had heard a noise in the lodge between four and five in the morning. On investigation he saw Pettit standing on the beams among some sheep coops.

"On going to him," Herriott goes on, "he asked me if I had seen anyone about. I said no. He then told me that he with Will Trigwell had just met ten or twelve Men who said to him that he was the B----r that betrayed the Berwick men and that the Men ran after him and he got into the Lodge to hide himself from them."

Herriott apparently believed Pettit's story and allowed him to go. Then he noticed that the fowls had gone too. He and his master, William Dray, then tracked Pettit across the heavily frosted ground and into Alfriston where they had him charged with theft.
Dray told the court: "I have missed a great many Fowls lately, some of Mr. Hilder's and others of my own".

The jury found Pettit not guilty.

There is no indication of who the men were who had chased Pettit at such an hour. Did Pettit not recognise them as men from the locality? And who were the Berwick men whom he had betrayed? One, perhaps two, of the Russells who appeared on other charges, worked at Berwick Court and Richard Saunders had stolen a lamb from there earlier in the year. Had Pettit denounced them? Sadly no evidence exists and the proceedings of this case are not recorded. It would have been interesting to have seen Will Trigwell's evidence: it is surprising that he was not charged along with Pettit.

1835

James Hawkett, a twenty-four year old carter, and John Levett, a labourer aged fourteen, were employed by John King at Berwick Court Farm. A fellow worker, James Russell, reported them to their employer for stealing 56lb of hay.

In court the two defendants said that King fed his horses on pollard and oats and that he would not allow them hay. Hawkett and Levett claimed to be trying to improve the animals' diet.

Sentencing them both to solitary confinement - Hawkett for one month, Levett for three days - the judge pointed out that the master not the servant made the rules. It was, he said,

> "an established rule in law that if a servant took his master's hay to feed his horses without leave, it was a felony. The master, not the servant, was to judge what horses should be allowed. If the latter [ie the servant] was dissatisfied with his place he might leave it."

1836

William Trigwell was fined £2 and costs for offences under the Game Laws - poaching "on the hill at Litlington".

"This Trigwell is, we understand," the Brighton Gazette reports, "one of the Alfriston Gang, who acquired the

the cognomen 'Trigger'. The two Huggetts have been taken up for sheep stealing and we believe that only one or two of this notorious gang is still at large."

What is interesting is how the notion of the gang continued so long after Collins' departure. Collins organised intensive and persistent crime in the locality. No other gang member could take over from him. Collins, in addition to whatever personal qualities he might have possessed, also had money, means of transport, storage capacity and outlets for corn and slaughtered sheep. The labourers who formed his gang had none of these advantages.

John and James Huggett, now living in Seaford, faced charges of assault and robbery, sheep stealing and animal maiming. At Sutton they had robbed Mr William Washer Woods of "three pieces of Current Copper Coin of this Realm called pence and Four pieces of the Current Copper Coin of this Realm called Halfpence".

From John King and Thomas Lidbetter, farming Berwick Court, they stole a ewe (£2/10); killed a lamb (30/-) and maimed two lambs (£3).

They were sentenced to death. At the end of the Assizes this sentence was commuted to transportation for life.

1837

Henry Page, a labourer, of Chapple Houses, Lullington, was sentenced to one week's imprisonment for the theft of "one fagot of the value of one penny", the property of Walter Woodhams of Lullington Court Farm.

John Reeds, still committing offences, was found guilty of stealing 100lb of coal (1/6) from Isaac Levey. He was given two weeks' hard labour.

How ever did Reeds manage to avoid transportation?

John Barber alias Russell stole two bushels of oats (6/-); one bushel of chaff (1d); one sack (2/-) belonging to John King at Berwick Court Farm, "... at the time of the said felony being a servant of the said John King."

He was imprisoned for six months.

There is no explanation for the alias.

Richard Ollive, a labourer, stole 26lbs of bacon (12/6); 4lb of cheese (2/1); two yards of muslin (10/-); 12 yards of calico (6/-); 6 yards of calico (3/-) belonging to George Bodle and 30lb of beef (20/-) from William Banks, now a butcher as well as a mealman and seller of beer, living in Market Cross House. Ollive had persuaded his lodger to go with him to Bodle's grocery and had taken out the goods under his smock frock. It can only be assumed that he made more than one journey.

Two weeks later he learnt that his house was to be searched and he hid some of the stolen goods in a hedge. The goods were found and identified by Bodle who prosecuted the culprit.

Ollive was transported for seven years.

James White, aged sixty-four, employed by John King at Berwick Court, broke into his master's cellar and stole a quart of beer (4d). He was given six months' hard labour, the first and last fortnight in solitary confinement.

It was the general rule of the court at Lewes, White was told, to transport felons who had been convicted on a previous occasion. In White's case the court took what it considered to be a humane stance in view of his age and ignored a previous unspecified conviction.

For the theft of three faggots valued at 4d from Charles Ade of Milton Court Farm, William Gosden was sent to prison for three weeks.

CONCLUSION

The preceding pages have described the majority of reported crimes and disorders in Alfriston and neighbourhood in the late Georgian period. There have been crimes of greed, need and revenge. With the exception of Stanton Collins, none of them made anyone rich. Indeed, most of them were quite modest offences. In criminal terms they were decidedly unambitious. The most serious were the fires and the motive for these in nearly every case was resentment, the desire to pay-out a master. Several of the cases for very minor offences - taking wood; poaching rabbits - were brought by farmers jealously possessive of their property rights. The Berwick Court case, where John King prosecuted his workers for feeding his horses contrary to his instructions, seems designed to do no more than prove that workers were not expected to presume to know as much as their masters.

But how much crime there was cannot be shown, cannot be known. As Fielding had observed, the chances of escaping detection were so high that crime was positively encouraged. The Alfriston Gang's offences went on for several years without a conviction. The ineffectiveness of the law-keeping machinery, prior to the introduction of a paid full-time police force, is demonstrated especially in those cases of arson where serious enquiries and large rewards had little or no effect. Thorncraft was arrested, it is safe to say, not because of meticulous policing by the constable but because he had so frequently signalled his intentions.

The legal system did, of course, uphold basic rights. There was no torture; no one could be held indefinitely without charge; there was the presumption of innocence; trials were fair. That said, the rule of law was backed up by the 'Bloody Code' which until the mid 1820s listed over two hundred capital offences. Yet even this was not enough to deter men from committing crimes. Sheep stealing until 1832 was a hanging matter; so was arson until 1838. Not that everyone convicted of such offences was automatically hanged. There was at the time, there had been for many years, a powerful distaste for hanging on the part of both judges and juries. As a consequence most of those capitally convicted - 85% is the estimate - had their sentences commuted. Hence, the vast numbers of those transported - 72,000 men and 12,000 women in the years between 1821 and 1840. The home prison system could not cope with such large numbers of convicts. Empty Australia could.

Poor Thorncraft. He might have been transported but he chose an unfortunate time for his crime. The Swing Riots were still fresh in the mind; there had been recent fires at Berwick Court and the Parsonage Barn; there had been attacks on Brooker's warehouse and doubtless other unrecorded arson attempts. Samuel Thorncraft could not have chosen a worse time for his offence.

In this period, Alfriston experienced particularly trying days. The law was powerless. Those acts of hooliganism in the mid-1820s; the 'riot' in front of Brooker's house; the activities of Collins' gang over several years. All suggest that what forces of law there were - constables, patrols, Prosecuting Society - were held in contempt.

Perhaps the village was unfortunate in having no lord of the manor or squire, someone owning all the property, making demands of his tenants and offering strong direction. Some villages were already promoting competition among labourers for the best-kept garden, the best-kept cottage. Awards were made in some places to large families who had not in the course of the year made claims upon the parish.

Even before the young Queen's accession, solid Victorian values - both good and bad - were already being forged in places like Ditchling and Glynde. The paternalism which encouraged these values would in certain quarters in our own time come to be sneered at. The claim would be that it encouraged a kind of forelock-tugging deference in the once sturdy, independent labourer. Yet at a time of great social, political and economic upheaval - with one kind of paternalism gone - the virtues of sobriety, responsibility and thrift needed to be reinforced among many who had never demonstrated either sturdiness or independence.

Such schemes of self-improvement were non-existent, however, in a village where the properties which the poor rented belonged to a variety of small local tradesmen, who expected profit from their property investments. In a time when labourers could afford only low rents, owners could do little in the way of repairs and maintenance. Competitions for best-kept cottages had no place here. There was no striving upwards. Instead there was merely a struggle to survive.

In the 1840s, Henry Pagden and other local farmers encouraged farm workers to form a Benefit Society from which, when ill, members could receive some financial help. The Society ultimately failed. Too many were said to draw sick benefit. Such a Society, of course, of which Pagden was chairman, was perhaps as much as anything intended to counter any wider movement of agricultural labourers such as that which Brooker was intent on promoting. A Society of this kind would also help to restore the farmers to their original position as masters of men. Finally, the Society's aim of relieving distress was to be achieved out of labourers' subscriptions rather than from money in the form of rates coming out of the pockets of the farmers.

Brooker, the stout radical, the powerful preacher, who went on to make two unsuccessful attempts to enter Parliament, had some effect upon crime though it cannot be measured. But any man who points out to the poor and landless that their lives can be improved, that there are ways of struggling against economic depression and deep injustice, makes some impression on those with little hope, those whose futures are bleak.

The long winter of the agricultural labourer would only end when the depression lifted and when the labour surplus no longer reduced his chances of regular work. And until then, rural crime would continue at a relatively high rate although not so seriously as in the late Georgian period.

As the century wore on, industry and work opportunities in Alfriston would decline yet further. Poverty would still be the daily lot of many. But the worst was over. There would be less crime. There was hope. There would be better times. But only after so many wasted years, so many damaged lives.

NOTES ON LOCATIONS

It may be that readers will wish to view some of the locations mentioned in the text. Not all of these require comment but some do, especially those which are not to be found on maps.

Alfriston

i) Waterloo Square

Market Cross House is where Stanton Collins lived and had his butcher's shop and slaughterhouse. In his time it was not a public house. Today it is The Smugglers Inn and it stands in the north-west corner of the Square.

Charles Brooker's house is located in the north-east corner of the Square. It is now known as Bank House.

ii) North Street

Banks' beer shop was in one of the cottages at the top of the street, just around the corner from the Square.

The Workhouse was further down the street. One of the cottages is called The Old Workhouse and it and one of the adjoining cottages housed the village poor prior to 1834. It was here that Jemima Coot most probably went after leaving Collins' service.

The brick-kiln cottage mentioned by one of the witnesses at Collins' trial was one of a pair known as Dene Cottages. These abut the main road going northwards out of the village. The high pavement outside the cottages is sometimes referred to as "down the bricks" and the field opposite is called Brick-Kiln Brook. In the last century a brick-kiln was found next to the cottages.

iii) Star Lane

Sevencrofts Barn is now the workshop of Lower's garage at the top of the lane. It was here where those who seceded from the chapel in 1831 held their meetings.

iv) The Twitten (Sussex word for alleyway)

Charles Brooker's shop which suffered from pilferers might have been at the top of the twitten on the corner of the High Street. Certainly George Woodhams, his son-in-law, had his grocery business here in 1841 and it is possible that Brooker handed it on to him.

The Chapel in which the riot occurred is in the twitten.

v) The Tye (Village Green)

The Parsonage Barn was behind the Church. Only parts of the wall remain. The area is now devoted to the Memorial Garden.

The National School which nearly fell victim to fire is now the village hall.

The tannery was behind the wall on the north side of the Tye. Two houses inside the wall - Tanneries and Farthings - and The Gun Room, were major parts of the tannery's buildings. Either Farthings or The Gun Room is likely to have been the warehouse which arsonists attacked unsuccessfully.

Lullington and Milton Street

i) Burlough Castle lies 300 or 400 yards beyond Milton Court Farm. Where the road bends sharply to the right, a grassy track lies straight ahead. It was here that Collins, Pearson and Huggett took their cart. Capper's barn was in the field on the left of the track.

ii) The Royal Oak and the three cottages adjoining it stood at what today is called Peachey's Corner. Nothing now remains of any of the buildings. The map used at Thorncraft's trial shows them straight ahead across Longbridge to the junction leading to Milton Street and Plonk Barn. The buildings stood on the east side of the road, just to the right of the track leading to Lullington Church.

Phillimore and Margary's map seems to show The Royal Oak in the road known as The Cathedral, that is, between Plonk Barn and Peachey's Corner. Was there a second building given the same name?

To add to the confusion, the present Sussex Ox in Milton Street bore the name The Royal Oak but this was after the years dealt with in this account.

iii) Levett's beer shop was in a large barn-like building - perhaps a terrace of two or three cottages - in Milton Street. Coming from Alfriston, instead of following the main road past the Sussex Ox, take the right fork at the junction. The building, now a private house, is on the left-hand side.

SOURCES

Bibliography

Annual Register, 1830; 1831
A Beckett, The Spirit of the Downs, Methuen, 1909
B Bushaway, By Rite: Custom, Ceremony and Continuity, Junction, 1982
William Cobbett, Rural Rides Vols 1 & 2, Culley,1909
J P D Dunbabin, Rural Discontent in 19th Century Britain, Faber, 1984
Edward B Ellman, Recollections of a Sussex Parson, Skeffington, 1912
C Emsley, Crime and Society in England, Longman, 1987
Emsley and Walvin, Artisans, Peasants and Proletarians, Croom Helm, 1985
Thomas Geering, Our Sussex Parish, Methuen, 1925
Richard Heath, The Victorian Peasant, Alan Sutton, 1989
Hobsbawm and Rudé, Captain Swing, Penguin, 1973
Thomas W Horsfield, A History of Sussex, 1835
Robert Hughes, The Fatal Shore, Pan, 1990
Elizabeth Longford, Wellington: Pillar of State, Panther, 1972
Macfarlane and Thomson, A Comprehensive History of England, Blackie, 1862
T R Malthus, Essay on Population, 1798
Florence Pagden, History of Alfriston, Combridges, 1895
A Cecil Piper, Alfriston, Muller, 1970
D Roberts, Paternalism in Early Victorian England, Croom Helm, 1979
J A Sharpe, Crime in Early Modern England, Longman, 1983
John Stevenson, Popular Disturbances in England, 1700-1870, Longman, 1979
W Swinfen and D Arscott, Guide to Hidden Sussex Day by Day, BBC Sussex Radio, 1987
G M Trevelyan, English Social History, Longman, 1944
Mary Waugh, Smuggling in Kent and Sussex 1700-1840, Countryside, 1985
Roger Wells, Popular Protest and Social Crime (Southern History, Vol 13), 1991

Manuscript Sources

(From East Sussex County Record Office, Lewes)
Baptismal, Marriage, Burial Registers 1815 - 1840
Minutes of Alfriston Chapel 1801 - 1840
Vestry Minutes 1820 - 1825
AMS 5774/4/5 (Marchant)
AMS 6294 (Brooker; Woodhams)

(From PRO, Kew)
Letters to Home Office
HO64/1; HO64/2; HO64/4

Contemporary Newspapers

(From ESCRO; British National Library, Colindale; University of Sussex Library; Brighton Reference Library)
The Times, Sussex Advertiser, Brighton Patriot, Brighton Gazette, Brighton Herald, Brighton Guardian.

Assizes

(From PRO, Chancery Lane)
Assi/35/272/5; Assi 35/276/5

Quarter Sessions

(From ESCRO)
QO/EW44-QO/EW 56; Q R/E79; Q R/E 826-827; Q R/E 809.

Reward Notices

(From PRO, Kew)
H064/2; HO64/4

Reports of Poor Law Commission
(From University of Sussex Library)
The Administration and Practical Operation of the Poor Law, 1834.
The Sanitary Condition of the Labouring Poor, 1837 - 1847.

Maps

(From ESCRO)
Section of Sussex Map, Margary and Phillimore, 1825
Hand-drawn Map, 1832 Trial, (SAS 61)

Illustrations

(By courtesy of the Rector and Churchwardens, St Andrew's Church, Alfriston)

Parsonage Barn, S H Grimm, 1787

By the same author
The Macaroni Dancers and Other Stories
Seaside Entertainment in Sussex
Sussex Disasters
Alfriston Past and Present
Alfriston Village School 1879 - 1909
Crime and Disorder in Late Victorian Alfriston
Previous offences: Crime in 19th Century Sussex
Sussex Tales of Mystery and Murder
Sussex Villains
Surrey Murder Casebook
Surrey Tales of Murder and Mystery
Surrey Villains
Essex Tales of Mystery and Murder
Essex Villains
Kent Murder Casebook
Kent Tales of Mystery and Murder
Kent Stories of the Supernatural
True Crime History: Sussex Murders
True Crimes from the Past: Kent